Dreams
And
Visions

By Kevin Etta Jr.

PREFACE

It is clear that the Lord would have his people to have a hearing ear and a seeing eye in this late hour. Hence, the central theme of this book is that of helping in some small way to give the saints of God a better understanding of the ways of the Spirit of God and the language by which He communicates with the human spirit within the context of dreams, visions and spiritual revelations.

Hosea 4:6 declares: "My people are destroyed for lack of knowledge." And in Proverbs 4:7 we are told: "Wisdom is the principal thing; therefore get wisdom: and with all thy getting get understanding."

It is our hope and prayer that the Lord will work into us both a desire and a capacity to develop a hearing ear and a seeing eye, to the intent that we might become more fully imbued with His presence and a sense and knowledge of His divine will in this day and hour.

Your servant,

Kevin Etta Jr.
December 2005

Table of Contents

Chapter One

The Mystical

For a wholesome consideration of any subject, a background study must be made into its basic components; the factors that are fundamental to its existence. Thus, when we marvel at the wonders of modern aviation, we can appreciate the labors of the background investigation and research that went into the development of aerodynamics. These principles now mastered and harnessed have launched us into this historic era of modern aviation technology.

We take for granted the benefits of the motor car and the comforts it affords, forgetting the research and study that went into the mastery of the principles of combustion and general mechanics. Excursions were made into the fundamental realms of these sciences in order to master the laws inherent in them. The results are abundantly advertised today.

Similarly, in considering this sacred spiritual trust of the Christian faith -- dreams and visions -- a journey must be made into the fundamental sphere of this operation of the Spirit to allow a proper understanding of the subject.

THE MYSTICAL REALM

We are entering into the fundamental sphere of the manifestations we know as dream and vision: the mystical realm. Never has the cry for understanding of this realm in general, and as it relates to Christianity in particular, been more pronounced than it is now. There has been much lost of the quality of Christian worship because these fundamentals are not given the primacy in Christian circles that existed in the days of our apostolic forbears. Secular humanism and rational thought have eaten deep into the fabric of religious doctrine and practice, and obscured much of what was formerly rudimentary Christian doctrine, practice and experience.

Christianity cannot exist in a virile and authentic form outside of its core essence: a faith and practice encompassing and comprehending in principle the varied forms, traditions and mysteries of the ancients of Biblical antiquity in both the Old and New Testaments. This is the faith we wish to presently explore.

The word 'mystical' answers to what originates from the mysterious and obscure realm of the spiritual. That mystical realm is intrinsic to -- and traverses -- all strata of human life and endeavor. A basic illustration of this is the fact that there is no person, religious or otherwise, who doesn't dream, or come under the influence of dreams in one way or another. In other words, whether or not we

6

believe in, or accept, the relevance of dreams, and visions, we are haunted by their prophetic, nightmarish, and sometimes uncannily graphic themes. Without question, we are, indeed, influenced to a greater or lesser degree by what emanates from the mystical realm as to our dreams. This mystical realm we wish to presently examine.

The book of Proverbs authored by Solomon is an invaluable part of the scriptural canon, and it was produced through the travails of this man as he journeyed through the different spheres of human wisdom, science, and industrial endeavor available to him at the time and he sought for a meaning to life. In the course of his search, Solomon ultimately stumbled upon the treasures of the precious wisdom and knowledge of God, much like Moses in the Midianite desert. Solomon, like Moses, apprehended and laid hold of the keys to this life as to the base atomic principles governing life in this world – and others; the mystical basis of life, ultimately gathered into and fully personified by the Christ of God.

Thus begins the preface to the book of Proverbs:

"The proverbs of Solomon the son of David, King of Israel; To know wisdom and instruction; to perceive the words of understanding; To receive the instruction of wisdom, justice, and judgment, and equity; To give subtility to the simple, to the young man knowledge and discretion." (Proverbs 1:1-4)

Solomon has said volumes in those four verses. We are going to take a little time to consider exactly what he is saying bearing in mind that we are making an inquiry into the atomic mystical principles at the very core of Christianity and its spring of manifestations. Let's begin with a paraphrase of those four verses.

> "The doctrine, and teaching of Solomon, the son of David, King of Israel. To educate and instruct a man in the true wisdom and learning. To the intent that he may apprehend the laws and principles governing the natural and the supernatural; the physical and the metaphysical. To impart to those without knowledge the true wisdom and to the novice the keys to this life."

That is perhaps, a simplified version of the preface to the book of Proverbs. The intention of the author is to introduce the reader to the base atomic principles foundational to the real knowledge of God and the mysteries of Christianity.

Remembering that Christianity is all about equipment, (see Ephesians 4:11-14) appreciate the fact that the book of Proverbs seeks to equip the reader to go out and dominate his natural and supernatural environment, which is, as I have said, what Christianity is all about.

From the very beginning, when God said "Let us make man in our image, after our likeness; and let them have dominion..." (Genesis 1:26) the spiritual antecedents of which Solomon's doctrine is a part, have been designed and intended to provide that equipment as to a foundational orientation in the mysteries that attend the embrace of Christianity.

> "A wise man will hear, and will increase in learning, and a man of understanding will attain unto wise counsels: To understand a proverb, and the interpretation; the words of the wise, and their dark sayings: The fear of the Lord is the beginning of knowledge; but fools despise wisdom and instruction." (Proverbs 1:5-7)

Again, we see that true wisdom is attained through taking account of the fundamental mystical principles intrinsic to the knowledge of God. Knowledge of God cannot be attained through secular, or even religious scholarship if it is undertaken according to the schedule of humanly devised systems of learning. Knowledge of God, true spiritual knowledge, will be acquired through experimental use and appreciation of the core elements at the root of such knowledge. This is why Solomon says "The fear of the Lord is the beginning of knowledge." The fear of the Lord in terms of practice and pursuit of the fundamentals of Godliness and the spiritual life.

THE WISDOM OF THE ANGELS

In contemplating the mystical realm and its composite mysteries from which spring the manifestations associated with real Christianity, we will have to come to grips with certain realities. The mysterious aspects of this realm have caused the foolish and ignorant to pass it off as nonsensical superstition. We know that the mystical, or spiritual realm, is one closely associated with symbolism. Popular concepts of dreams, visions, prophecies, signs and portents, have relegated them to the position of superstitious distractions essentially embellished with picturesque emblems and imagery, largely out of tune with the totally rational mind.

But when we take a look at this issue from God's vantage point of spiritual realities, we discover several concepts relative to the acute symbolism of the mystical realm to be consistent with the spiritual nature of divinely constituted realities.

> "To understand a proverb, and the interpretation; the words of the wise, and their dark sayings." (Proverbs 1:6)

> A paraphrase of this would be:

> "An introduction to the accumulated encyclopedia of spiritual knowledge; the language of angels, and spirits."

This is what the book of Proverbs is all about. It is to give the reader a course in spiritual diction -- "the words of the wise, and their dark sayings."

Many Christians do not realize that there is a system or cipher of spiritual knowledge and information and a method of decoding and deciphering spiritual messages. This spiritual system is indigenous or native to the spiritual realm, the mystical realm. This spiritual system (code or cipher) is germane to all spiritual communications.

In Proverbs 1:20-23, we read about the all-encompassing significance of this spiritual system:

> "Wisdom crieth without; She uttereth her voice in the streets; she crieth in the chief place of concourse, in the openings of the gates; in the city she uttereth her words, saying, How long, ye simple ones will ye love simplicity? and the scorners delight in their scorning, and fools hate knowledge? Turn you at my reproof: behold, I will pour out my spirit unto you, I will make known my words unto you."

This spiritual system of knowledge "cries in the chief place of concourse." In other words, on the one hand it is competing today for attention among the more popular kinds of learning in the secular and academic spheres; it competes with the more mundane kinds of learning, in the scramble for mysticism and the occult. On the other hand, it competes "in the opening of the gates" – that is, in the strongholds of the mind where the Spirit speaks natively through our human spirit in an attempt to get our attention and provide guidance and direction in everyday life, much of which communication occurs unbeknownst to us and is mostly ignored and dismissed. Amid all this, and in spite of our ignorance, the divinely constituted spiritual knowledge and wisdom sits atop and takes a pre-eminent position of significance if men can but humble themselves and learn.

> "Turn you at my reproof: behold, I will pour out my spirit unto you, I will make known my words unto you."

This spring of mystical composition -- these "heavens" -- will be opened to the humble by the operation of the Spirit. Here, Solomon speaks of the outpouring of the Spirit in connection with the mysterious much the same way the prophet Joel, and later the apostle Peter, speak of the latter-day outpouring in connection with the supernatural manifestations:

> "And it shall come to pass in the last days, saith God, I will pour out of my spirit upon all flesh: and your sons and your daughters shall prophesy, and your young men shall see visions, and your old men shall dream dreams." (Acts 2:17)

The outpouring of the Holy Spirit, generally described as the Pentecostal experience, was to bring to the forefront the obscure realm of the mystical to the extent that the spiritual system of divine wisdom and power might have controlling interest and expression in a people God would call His own.

When we look at the life and ministry of the prophet Ezekiel, we see a man upon whom and to whom the obscure mystical realm was opened in generous measure. Time and again, spiritual realities were displayed before him in confusing and sometimes complicating symbolism difficult to understand.

The book opens with an account of how his extraordinary intercourse with the mystical realm began.

> "Now it came to pass in the thirtieth year, in the fourth month, as I was among the captives by the river of Chebar, that the heavens were opened, and I saw visions of God." (Ezekiel 1:1)

What is presented to us here is the case of man troubled by the distressing conditions of the captive state of his native people. However, despite his passion he is unfamiliar with the base atomic conditions responsible for the captivity. Unfamiliar that is, until the "heavens are opened" unto him and he begins to see "visions of God." Now he is apprised of things in an objective way and in accordance with the elemental wisdom at the root of the situation. He has a channel through which he might receive insight into the mysteries of the spiritual world as regards the position of Israel in the sphere of God's plans for them.

THE SUPERSITIONS OF THE ANCIENTS

Ancient traditions demonstrate that much attention and respect were accorded the mystical experiences of dream and vision. Omens, signs, and the like, were considered with the utmost reverence as sacred communications from

God and His angelic ministers. The destinies of individuals and nations were believed to be determined by these experiences, and it was believed that wars were won, and lost, on account of them.

There is ample proof from the Scriptures confirming the place of these phenomena in the arena of faith and worship. A good example is the story of Jacob's dream of the ladder that stood upon the earth and reached unto the heavens providing a thoroughfare for ministering spirits that ascended and descended the ladder.

> "And he lighted upon a certain place, and tarried there all night, because the sun was set; and he took of the stones of that place and put them for his pillows, and lay down in that place to sleep. And he dreamed, and behold a ladder set up on the earth, and the top of it reached to heaven: and behold, the angels of God ascending and descending on it." (Genesis 28:11, 12)

Reading that passage further, we discover that Jacob received a solemn promise from the Lord concerning his inheritance. This promise was the central theme underlying the deliberate undertakings the Lord made in his behalf throughout the course of Jacob's life. In fact, further consideration of this dream in the light of a parallel illustration drawn by our Lord Jesus Christ shows the dream of Jacob to be central and prophetic to certain themes enshrining the noblest concepts of the Christian faith.

14

Jacob dreamed of a ladder, a stairway that connected the heaven with the earth, and traversed by all the glorious traffic of celestial grace. In other words, God would provide a means by which unregenerate man could attain to salvation and virtue. Christ, as the stairway or conduit by whom fallen man could receive the abundant grace of the lofty God, makes a reference to Jacob's dream alluding to himself as the manifestation of that divine prophecy. Hear him speaking in John 1:51.

> "Truly, truly, I say unto you, you will see heaven opened, and the angels of God ascending and descending upon the son of man."

Here we see, represented by the dream of Jacob, the case so plainly stated by our Lord, as to the manifestation of God's grace springing from the mystical realm: "You will see heaven opened, and the angels of God ascending and descending upon the son of man." The statement, indeed, properly refers to Christ Jesus, himself -- the Way, the Truth, and the Life. But the principle can be carried further to describe the opening of the obscure mystical realm or "heavens" upon man by the ministering angels bringing dream upon dream, vision upon vision, to bear on the recipient of God's grace. This is, in fact, the work of the angels. They are "ministering spirits sent forth to minister for them who shall be the heirs of salvation." (Hebrews 1:14)

This fact was inscrutably accepted by the ancients, and is very apparent from all Biblical accounts. Dreams and visions were looked upon as sacred and treasured communications from the divine for the assistance of those who are the beneficiaries of God's grace.

THE ALLEGORY OF NEBUCHADNEZZAR'S COURT

I remember being in attendance at the Sunday service of a well-known Pentecostal Church in Calabar, when the sermonizing pastor made a remark about dreams that relegated them to a position of puerile superstition. I remember feeling sorry for the pastor as I imagined how little he must know of the Christian faith that he preached.

To many people, dreams and their consideration form part of the broad interest and distractions of popular mystical attentions such as horoscopes and the like. Dreams do, indeed, form a part of the array of mysterious and paranormal phenomena. In fact, they hold a very central position in this sphere. From a Judeo-Christian perspective, strictly speaking, dreams and visions form a crucial part of the bedrock of the practical and original worship of God.

From the story of Daniel's rise to prominence in the court of a heathen king, an interesting allegory can be found that sets the concept of dreams in its place in the mystical sphere.

Nebuchadnezzar was a heathen king that customarily held more than a healthy regard for the mystical realm and the possibilities it offered. He accumulated a store of mystical talent in an elaborate Court filled with counselors and spiritual advisers.

In chapter 2 of the book of Daniel, we read that Nebuchadnezzar had a dream, a particularly provocative dream that could not be fathomed by anyone in his mystical college.

> "And in the second year of the reign of Nebuchadnezzar, Nebuchadnezzar dreamed dreams, wherewith his spirit was troubled, and his sleep brake from him. Then the king commanded to call the magicians, and the astrologers, and the sorcerers, and the Chaldeans, for to shew the king his dreams. So they came and stood before the king." (Daniel 2:1, 2)

Bear in mind that according to the narrative of that entire chapter, the king's counselors were unable to proffer a solution or an interpretation to his riddle -- except Daniel, of whom it is said in chapter 1:17 that: "As for these four children, God gave them knowledge and skill in all learning and wisdom: and Daniel had understanding in all visions and dreams."

The Court of Nebuchadnezzar, populated as it was, with magicians, astrologers, and sorcerers, represents and symbolizes the mystical realm comprised of an admixture of spirits of varying denomination, purpose and messaging -- corresponding to the aforementioned members of Nebuchadnezzar's Court.

But in the midst of this mesh of competing spiritual forces and messaging -- just as Daniel stood out and attained distinction, the matter of dreams and visions from God stands superior to others. This is the allegory of Nebuchadnezzar's court.

Daniel personifies the spirit of divine wisdom and revelation that operates amid the admixture of paranormal phenomena in mystical realm and that supersedes all in clarity and power.

There is a divine wisdom and power that exists spiritually as communicated and transmitted from the realm of the mysterious and that compares in form, if not in substance, with what is purely mystical in nature. An attempt to divest Christianity of its true, original and native mystical ingredient will leave it a shell of its true self – a mere belief system, and one that lacks power and conviction. It will also lack the reality of God amply proven and demonstrated by the template of the Pentecostal outpouring of the Holy Spirit.

Solomon spoke of this in Proverbs 1:23, which runs parallel to the New Testament principles echoed and re-echoed by Joel and Peter respectively.

"Turn you at my reproof: behold, I will pour out my spirit unto you, I will make known my words unto you."

And from Joel 2:28 and Acts 2:17.

"And it shall come to pass in the last days, saith God, I will pour out of my spirit upon all flesh: and your sons and your daughters shall prophesy, and your young men shall see visions, and your old men shall dream dreams."

How is it that we can proclaim ourselves to be Full Gospel -- and for some, Pentecostal -- and make so much of the gift of speaking in tongues (as a for instance), and yet conceptualize so little on fundamental attributes of Pentecostal spirituality like dreams and visions?

From the allegory of Nebuchadnezzar's court, we see that the subject of dreams, visions and their interpretation takes its character from and possesses a commonality with the realm or sphere of that which is basically mystical in nature. From this context, the subject of dreams and visions achieves prominence and pre-eminence as representing a distinctly peculiar manifestation of the grace of God.

Using Daniel as the symbolism, a comparison is again drawn in the text of Daniel 5:11-12 between the ministry of God's grace through the agency of dreams, visions and their interpretations, and the other elements of the mystical Court -- sorcery, magic, astrology, etc.

"There is a man in thy kingdom, in whom is the spirit of the holy gods, and in the days of thy father light and understanding and wisdom, like the wisdom of the gods, was found in him; whom the king, Nebuchadnezzar, thy father...made *master* of the magicians, astrologers, chaldeans, and soothsayers, forasmuch as an excellent spirit, and knowledge and understanding, interpreting of dreams, and shewing of hard sentences and dissolving of doubts, were found in the same Daniel...now let Daniel be called, and he will shew the interpretation."

What a fitting and exhaustive description of the significance of dreams and visions. Daniel here allegorically depicts the superior nature of the agency of dreams. This is also an exhaustive resume of what this manifestation is. We see that the agency of dreams is a mystical phenomenon. We see that it represents a wisdom, intelligence, and communication far beyond the compare of the purely mystical. We see that the agency deals in an in-depth fashion with the mysterious. We also see that this agency is bequeathed to the sons of God as one among many a divine gift and manifestation, and – even among sons of God -- there are degrees to the agency and expression of this gift, with the unsanctified and ungodly witnessing a lesser degree, whilst the sanctified have a deeper penetration into the heart of mind of God, and hence a fuller expression and manifestation of the gift.

To those who would be truly spiritual, let them repent, renounce sin and the world, be converted unto the salvation of Jesus Christ, and receive the Holy Ghost that they may be ushered into an odyssey of spiritual realities.

There is a right and proper gift of dreams and visions from the spirit of God liaising the spiritual man with the spiritual realm, the mystical realm, and beyond compare of the other powers of clairvoyance that form a part of the mystical spectrum.

The concept of dreams seems fraught with much diffuse opinion due to its obscure, confusing and sometimes perplexing manifestation. But dreams are not really as diffuse as they may seem. There is, as I said earlier, a spiritual system. There is a system of mystical engineering that affects directly the manifestation of dreams and visions. This system of mystical engineering forms the high level image that mirrors the kaleidoscopic network of dreams, visions, prophecies, and other mysteries onto the canvas of our minds and our spiritual horizons. The spiritual system is known as Vision and Prophecy, a term that can be found in Daniel 9:24.

> "Seventy weeks are determined upon thy people and upon thy holy city, to finish the transgression, and to make an end of sins, and to make reconciliation for iniquity, and to bring in everlasting righteousness, and to seal up *the vision and prophecy,* and to anoint the most holy. "

At this time we are not concerned with the prophetic significance of the Seventy Weeks of Daniel. But we wish to point out that, among other things, this was to be a period of full disclosure in terms of the application and fulfillment of the Scriptures of the prophets (the vision and prophecy) -- the completion of which would signify the loosening of all the sealed mysteries of the prophets (see Revelation 10:7). Vision and Prophecy therefore signifies an array of prophetic insights into past, present, and future history. Or, if you like…

THE HEAVENLY ALMANAC

"Now it came to pass in the thirteenth year, in the fourth month, in the fifth day of the month, as I was among the captives by the river of Chebar, that the heavens were opened and I saw visions of God."(Ezek. 1:1)

Now, let it be held that the opening of the heavens corresponds to the insights into the mystical realm that we know as dream and vision. Hence, when we speak of the "heavens" we are speaking of the mystical realm of which we have said much already.

In the 10th chapter of Daniel, he is accosted by the archangel Gabriel who makes certain salutary remarks and then proceeds to present Daniel with an overview of future historical events with respect to the kingdoms of Persia, Greece, and Rome. This special presentation commences at Daniel 10:21 through Daniel 11:1-45. In Daniel 10:21, the angel makes a fantastic statement in connection with, and prefatory to, the presentation that proceeds thereafter.

"But I will shew (or expound to) thee that

which is noted (or written) in the scripture (book or scroll) of truth."

As we have said, the angel proceeds to expound to Daniel chronicles of future events as yet unwritten -- at least, by man. But he referred to a book or scroll of truth. What book is that which might hold the chronicles of future events as yet undisclosed to and unwritten by man?

David answers this question for us in Psalm 102:25-26, and his answer is subsequently echoed by the apostle Paul in Hebrews 1:10-12.

"Of old hast thou laid the foundation of the earth: and the heavens are the work (scripture) of thy hands. They shall perish, but thou shalt endure: yea, all of them shall wax old like a garment; as a vesture shalt thou change them, and they shall be changed."

These are the "stellar etchings" if you like, where God imprinted the orders of the dispensations down to their minutest details. In Psalm 102:24, before the description in the passage quoted above, the Lord Jesus speaks prophetically through His servant David about his decease in the middle of his provisional seventy year life-span at an age of thirty-three and one-half years: "I said, O my God, take me not away in the midst of my days: thy years are throughout all generations." Jesus says this because he anticipates from Vision and Prophecy (the almanac) that his life will be abruptly ended in the middle of his years on earth as an atonement for our sins. David throws more light on this in Psalm 89.

David sees in vision the promise of God to establish the throne of His Christ forever. He sees it established unchangeable in one instance. In another, he sees an entirely different thing as he beholds in the vision the Christ whom the Lord promises glory and honor, suddenly becoming the victim of shame and scorn.

> "Then thou spakest in a vision to thy holy one, and saidst, I have laid help upon one that is mighty, I have exalted one chosen out of the people. I have found David my servant; with my holy oil have I anointed him... my covenant will I not break, nor alter the thing that is gone out of my lips. Once I have sworn by my holiness that I will not lie unto David. His seed shall endure forever, and his throne as the sun before me. It shall be established forever as the moon, and as a faithful witness in heaven (from here begins the contrast that suddenly appeared to David in the heavenly vision). But thou hast cast off and abhorred, thou hast been wroth with thine anointed. Thou hast made void the covenant of thy servant: thou hast profaned his crown by casting it to the ground. Thou hast broken down all his hedges; thou hast brought his strongholds to ruin. All that pass by the way spoil him: he is a reproach to his neighbors. Thou hast

set up the right hand of his adversaries; thou hast made all his enemies to rejoice. Thou hast also turned the edge of his sword, and not made him to stand in the battle. Thou hast made his glory to cease, and cast his throne down to the ground. The days of his youth hast thou shortened: thou hast covered him with shame." (Psalm 89:19, 20, 34-45)

Among other things about this remarkable scripture are the symbolisms of sun and moon in verses 36 and 37 used in connection with the glory and majesty of Christ being established unchangeable "as a faithful witness in heaven." (Verse 37).

David in Psalm 8:3-6 gives a similar impression where the same symbolisms are used in the same sense.

"When I consider thy heavens (Vision and Prophecy, the almanac) the work of thy fingers (the scripture alluded to by Gabriel in Daniel 10:21) The moon and stars, which thou hast ordained; what is man, that thou art mindful of him? and the son of man that thou visitest him? For thou hast made him a little lower than the angels, and hast crowned him with glory and honor."

Perhaps you've begun to grasp the fact David was not at all referring to the physical heavens enshrining the sun, the moon, and the stars. But he was gazing at the heavenly almanac and beholding in vision the glory and honor God had kept for his Christ (His corporate Christ: Jesus, as head, in unity with the Church, his body.) displayed in all the resplendent glory of picturesque imagery and emblematic symbolism.

Paul also refers to this vision of David, and applies it to New Testament doctrine in Hebrews 2: 6-9. Also, in Revelation 12:1-5 fuller use is made of this symbolism in John's cryptic descriptions of the final titanic struggles between the saints and the devil preceding their triumphal assumption to glory.

> "And there appeared a great wonder in heaven; a woman clothed with the sun, and the moon under her feet, and upon her head a crown of twelve stars: and she being with child cried, travailing in birth, and pained to be delivered. And there appeared another great wonder in heaven; and behold a great red dragon, having seven heads and ten horns, and seven crowns upon his heads. And his tail drew a third part of the stars of heaven, and did cast them to the earth: and the dragon stood before the woman which was ready to be delivered, for to devour her child as soon as it was born. And she brought forth a man-child, who was to rule all nations with a rod of iron: and her child was caught up unto God, and to his throne."

Aptly spoken by the august apostle. Truly, what

wonders to behold when one gazes upon the panoramic pageantry of the Vision and Prophecy, inexorably drawn into its depths; traversing the length and breadth of its labyrinthine theatricals! It is vision upon vision, and dream upon dream, in the almost endless expanse; the measureless screen of picturesque imagery and emblematic symbolism.

This is the "book of truth" spoken of and administered by the angels. This is the heavenly scroll stretched out amid eternity's expanse to govern and control the administration of divine grace in the kingdoms of men.

David again speaks in Psalm 40:7-8 having gazed upon inestimable treasure -- the heavenly portents of the advent of Christ -- displayed in the cryptic visionary representations of the mystical annals. He speaks prophetically of the resolute Christ desirous to perform the historic pilgrimage of the incarnation based on the script recorded in the "book."

> "Then said I, lo, I come: in the volume of the
> book it is written of me, I delight to do thy will, O
> my God: yea, Thy law is within my heart."

Christ came to act out his pre-destiny as recorded in the "book." Every other man must act out his own part of that script. David, rapt in his vision, again bears this out in Psalm 139:14-16.

> "I will praise thee; for I am fearfully and
> wonderfully made: marvelous are thy works; and

27

that my soul knoweth right well. My substance was not hid from thee, when I was made in secret, and curiously wrought in the lowest parts of the earth. Thy eyes did see my substance, yet being unperfect; *and in thy book all my members were written*, which in continuance were fashioned, when as yet there was none of them."

And in the most graphic of David's sermons on the almanac we have the familiar words of Psalm 19:1-5.

"The heavens declare the glory of God; and the firmament sheweth (describes) his handiwork. Day unto day uttereth speech (doctrine), and night unto night sheweth knowledge (describes the cycles of God's dealings with men in cryptic dreams and visions). There is no speech, or language, where their voice is not heard. Their line (their control, direction, and influence) is gone out through all the earth, and their words to the end of the world. In them hath he set a tabernacle for the sun, (he begins to use the symbolic language of the inheritance) which is as a bridegroom coming out of his chamber, and rejoiceth as a strong man to run a race."

David clearly postulates that the heavens that opened to Ezekiel granting visions of God, have been so designed of God to exact complete control in influencing and directing the affairs of men. This is Vision and Prophecy, which according to Daniel 9:24 was to have validation

28

until the full disclosure and fulfillment of the prophetic mysteries of the Scriptures. The expiry of the present Vision and Prophecy, "almanac" or "heavens" is anticipated to come at the Consummation and the establishing of the Kingdom when there has been a full, complete and exhaustive appreciation, understanding, interpretation, fulfillment, manifestation, and application of the written scriptures of the prophets. Then this "book" or "scroll" of the almanac is to be rolled up making way for a new dispensation of similar engineering to govern the ages of kindness to roll us forward through the millennial reign of Christ (and beyond) when he shall have "put down all rule and authority."

This thought is aptly borne out in the prophecy of Isaiah 34:4.

> "And all the host of heaven shall be dissolved, and the heavens shall be rolled together as a scroll: and all their host shall fall down, as the leaf falleth off from the vine, and as a falling fig from the fig tree."

Also, in Isaiah 51:6.

> "Lift up your eyes to the heavens, and look upon the earth beneath: for the heavens shall vanish away like smoke..."

John's visions in the Revelation have much bearing on this. Revelation 6:12-14.

"And I beheld when he had opened the sixth seal, and, lo, there was a great earthquake; and the sun became black as sackcloth of hair, and the moon became as blood; And the stars of heaven fell unto the earth, even as a fig tree casteth her untimely figs, when she is shaken of a mighty wind. And the heaven departed as a scroll when it is rolled together; and every mountain and island were moved out of their places."

Unable to resist the temptation, allow me to present once again Paul's magnificent rendition of the latter part of David's 102nd Psalm.

"And, Thou, Lord, in the beginning hast laid the foundation of the earth; and the heavens are the works of thine hands: They shall perish; but thou remainest; and they shall wax old as doth a garment; And as a vesture shalt thou fold them up, and they shall be changed..." (Hebrews 1:10-12)

Speaking conclusively about the time of full disclosure and expiry of this vision and prophecy or "mystery" as he calls it, John makes his case in the vision of Revelation 10:7.

"But in the days of the voice of the seventh angel, when he shall begin to sound, the mystery of God should be finished, as he hath declared to his servants the prophets."

In other words, at the time of the last trump, at the consummation of all things and the dawn of the Kingdom

Age, the mystery of God as declared to His servants the prophets would have reached its expiry, and shall be changed.

In closing this chapter, here's a recap of our discussions.

1. We have attempted to introduce the basic constituency (and its constituent factors) of the spiritual life in relation to Christianity.

2. There is a mystical realm also known as the "spiritual world" and the "heavens".

3. Amid the myriad generic mystical and occult phenomena, the divine gift of dreams and visions stands pre-eminent as an agency of salvation, deliverance and wisdom; whilst possessing -- and being possessed of -- the same native and generic qualities with others as to its spiritual denominator which is the mystical realm.

4. This gift of dreams and visions is the product of a fellowship and insight into the sacred mystical annals of the almanac, known as Vision and Prophecy.

5. The treasures of this heavenly 'book' are mostly hidden and obscured from the sons of Adam, except those like Ezekiel and other prophets and apostles -- down to the present -- to whom the "heavens" are opened to behold "visions of God."

6. This heavenly almanac governs the plan and

purposes of God for all creation, and is administered by the Lord and His angels through the agencies of dreams, visions, prophecies, revelations, etc.

Chapter Two

Dreams and Visions

Most people are familiar with dreams as experiences they have when they are asleep. Suddenly, they are awakened from slumber to discover they have transacted certain business while they slept. With visions, it's typical for one to be -- at the very least -- partially awake, and sometimes wide awake, whilst in a vision and sometimes in a trance receiving messages from God.

There are also cases where the trance-like state of the vision is so deep that the person is unconscious, hence oblivious of his/her immediate surroundings, and thoroughly overwhelmed by the power of the vision.

At other times, one may also enter the trance-like state of deep vision through a dream or dreams. Many a time people enter a powerful vision through their dreams. In fact, the two separate experiences of dream and vision though distinct, are not wholly disparate, but very closely related.

THE PLACE OF DREAMS IN CHRISTIANITY

At the instance of the historic outpouring of the Holy Ghost at Pentecost as narrated in *Acts of the Apostles*, there was endowment of power from above on the disciples and apostles of Christ. This experience unlocked the sphere of the heavens to the saints to the extent that they instantly became spiritual men and women experiencing spontaneous ecstasies and manifestations of the Spirit. They spoke with new tongues and prophesied, at once attracting the ire of a skeptical indigent crowd. In response to the curious onlookers' words, Peter stood out from the midst of his brethren and spoke as recorded in Acts 2:15-17.

> "For these are not drunken, as ye suppose seeing it is but the third hour of the day. But this is that which was spoken by the prophet Joel; And it shall come to pass in the last days, saith God, I will pour out of my spirit upon all flesh: and your sons and your daughters shall prophecy, and your young men shall see visions, and your old men shall dream dreams."

Throughout Judeo-Christian antiquity, spanning the Old and New Testaments, the manifestation of dreams has been paramountly associated with the operation of the Holy Ghost. In the earliest Biblical record, the book of Genesis, we have the popular account of the dreams of Joseph, himself known as the dreamer. Interestingly, it was Joseph's dreams that seem to have cost him all the trouble he got himself into. Let us consider two of his dreams.

> "And Joseph dreamed a dream, and he told it his brethren: and they hated him yet the more.

34

And he said unto them, Hear, I pray you, this dream which I have dreamed: For, behold, we were binding sheaves in the field, and, lo, my sheaf arose, and also stood upright; and, behold, your sheaves stood round about, and made obeisance to my sheaf. And his brethren said unto him, shalt thou indeed reign over us? Or shalt thou indeed have dominion over us? And they hated him yet the more for his dreams, and his words. And he dreamed yet another dream, and told it his brethren, and said, Behold, I have dreamed a dream more; and, behold, the sun and the moon and the eleven stars made obeisance to me. And he told it to his father, and to his brethren; and his father rebuked him, and said unto him, what is this dream that thou hast dreamed? Shall I and thy mother and thy brethren indeed come to bow down ourselves to thee to the earth."

We see that Joseph had two relatively simple dreams in terms of their meaning. They spoke of his ultimate material pre-eminence over his brethren and his parents. They evidently caused much disquiet in the family, a fact that led to the performance of that dastardly act on the part of his brethren. Joseph was sold into slavery in Egypt, never again to be free -- but for God's infinite mercy and grace.

Miraculously, after several harrowing years of

incarceration in an Egyptian jail, he suddenly finds himself free and promoted to the premiership of Egypt, at the time the most powerful nation in the world.

Joseph eventually presides over the economic affairs of Egypt in particular, and the region in general; and yes, his brethren do bow to him, and his father too. Joseph's dream was divinely ordained to try and sustain him until he beheld the advent of God's purposes. Joseph, a deeply spiritual man, walked hand in hand with his dreams until he was successfully escorted to apprehend his fullness.

We will now examine a case from the scriptures of a person entering a vision through his dream. In other words, a dream that is really a vision.

> "In the first year of Belshazzar, King of Babylon, Daniel had a dream and visions of his head upon his bed: then he wrote the dream, and told the sum of the matters. Daniel spoke and said, I saw in my vision by night and behold the four winds of the heaven strove upon the great sea..." (Daniel 7:1-2)

In the subsequent narrative, we see a graphic description of four hideous beasts appearing one after the other, each more terrible than the one preceding. There was comparative havoc wreaked by each beast upon men until the Ancient of days came to sit in judgment and destroy the dominion of these beasts. At this point, we see something remarkable. It becomes clear from verse 15 of the same chapter that Daniel is not just in an ordinary dream, but has entered into a deep trance-like vision.

> "I Daniel was grieved in my spirit in the midst of my body, and the visions of my head troubled me. I came near unto one of them that stood by, and asked him the truth of all this; so he told me, and made me know the interpretation of these things."

What follows is a comprehensive explanation of the vision by the angel within the same composite vision. The result of this being that upon awaking there is a detailed composition in the mind of Daniel of what would otherwise have been a very confusing and upsetting affair. This is an example of a very forceful dream that is, as we said, actually a vision. Such experiences are usually the perquisites of those who have the dream-gift at an advanced level. They are uncommon.

Recently, I had such an experience. Having retired for the night and fallen into a deep sleep, I was taken to a place where an angel gave me a presentation on many divine spiritual truths. All the time the angel was speaking, I was writing down his words on a piece of parchment whilst I uttered periodic exclamation at the wondrous truths expounded to me by the angel. Upon conclusion of the presentation, I was instructed to rehearse everything I had been taught so as not to forget upon awaking in my body. I began to rehearse everything on the parchment whilst I arched myself closer and closer to my body which lay on the bed, until finally -- I jumped into my body and awoke. This is another example of entering into a trance-like vision through a dream.

In *Acts of the Apostles*, we have an example of an ordinary vision, i.e., a vision that appears while the recipient is in the conscious state. This is the story of how the Lord appeared to Ananias, and persuaded him to go and pray for the newly converted Saul of Tarsus.

"And there was a certain disciple at Damascus, named Ananias; and to him said the Lord in a vision, Ananias, and he said, Behold, I am here Lord. And the Lord said unto him, Arise, and go into the street which is called straight, and inquire in the house of Judas for one called Saul, of Tarsus: for, behold, he prayeth, And hath seen in a vision a man named Ananias coming in, and putting his hand on him, that he might receive his sight. Then Ananias answered, Lord, I have heard by many of this man, how much evil he hath done to thy saints at Jerusalem. And here he hath authority from the Chief Priests to bind all that call on thy name. But the Lord said unto him, Go thy way, for he is a chosen vessel unto me, to bear my name before the Gentiles and kings, and the children of Israel: for I will shew him how great things he must suffer for my name's sake. And Ananias went his way, and entered into the house and putting his hands on him said, Brother Saul, the Lord, even Jesus, that appeared unto thee in the way as thou camest, hath sent me, that thou mightest receive thy sight, and be filled with the Holy Ghost. And immediately there fell from his eyes as it had been scales: and he received sight forthwith, and arose, and was baptized." (Acts 9:10-18)

We see here how an otherwise impossible situation was made possible by the Lord's intervention through a vision. In the first instance, Ananias would never have been persuaded to take what seemed to him a senseless risk in attempting to visit the man Saul of Tarsus, were it not for the urgency of the medium used by Jesus to communicate with him.

Secondly, Saul himself, while praying, saw in a vision a man named Ananias coming to pray for him that he might receive his sight. The net result of the two experiences was that Saul received both his healing and the gift of the Holy Ghost. Usually, but not always, an open vision of this sort may have an accelerated result. It normally signifies urgency and imminence.

Another example of a vision of this sort can be found in the story of how Peter made the acquaintance of Cornelius, a Roman centurion. Apparently, an angel of God had appeared to Cornelius in a vision and advised him to send for a man name Simon Peter. The angel further gave him accurate directions as to the man's whereabouts. Cornelius dispatched an envoy immediately to seek out this Simon Peter. From Acts 10:9 onward our story continues...

"On the morrow, as they went on their journey, and drew nigh unto the city, Peter went up on the housetop to pray about the sixth hour: And he became very hungry, and would have eaten: but while they made ready, he fell into a trance, and saw heaven opened, and a certain vessel descending unto him, as it had been a great sheet knit at the four corners, and let down to the earth: wherein were all manner of four-footed beasts of the earth, and wild beasts, and creeping things, and fouls of the air. And there came a voice to him, Rise, Peter; kill, and eat. But Peter said, Not so, Lord; for I have never eaten anything that is common or unclean. And the voice spoke unto him the second time, what God hath cleansed, that call not thou common. This was done thrice: and the vessel was received up again into heaven. Now, while Peter doubted in himself what this vision which he had seen should mean, behold, the men which were sent from Cornelius had made inquiry for Simon's house, and stood before the gate, And called, and asked whether Simon, which was surnamed Peter, were lodged there. While Peter thought on the vision, the spirit said unto him, Behold, three men seek thee. Arise therefore, and get thee down, and go with them, doubting nothing: for I have sent them." (Acts 10:9-20)

Reading that story to the end you will see the fantastic run of events that led up to Peter's instrumentality in Cornelius' entire household receiving the Holy Ghost.

One general factor underscoring each of the experiences of dreams and visions we have enumerated is that the Spirit is in action. He is always seen to be actively orchestrating the run of events surrounding the manifestations, albeit in different degrees of urgency.

For Joseph's dream, the urgency was much less as it would take years before he saw the fulfillment of his dreams. In the case of Ananias', Paul's, Cornelius', and Peter's visions the urgency is much more evident as something was already happening, or about to happen, at the time the visions manifested.

There are also times, as in the case of the dreams of Pharaoh's chief baker and cupbearer who briefly visited Joseph in the Egyptian prison, when dreams may have pronounced urgency in terms of their immediate fulfillment. Remember that within a period of 3 days both men received the fulfillment of their dreams; one was hanged, while the other was restored back to his office.

In the case of the two prior examples (the one from Daniel, and the other personal) of going into deep trance either through a dream or through an open vision, the emphasis is not necessarily that of urgency, or the lack of (it may well include both factors), but of detail. Deep trance is significant because it affords the man an opportunity to see things and accumulate information in detail. It is a reconnaissance operation designed to afford an in-depth examination of the situation.

Another very good example from the scriptures of deep trance is the book of Revelation authored by the apostle John. Throughout the entire experience John was in very deep trance. It is possible that the experience itself was a rolling succession of trances in different segments within a set period; one after the other. But the fact remains that that kind of detailed examination and observation can only be done in deep trance. Also, like I have said, the elements of urgency -- and the lack of it -- are also evident in that vision. But again, the emphasis is on the detail.

The place of dreams and visions in Christianity is evident from tradition, experience, and Biblical history. In the Old Testament prophetic books, we are repeatedly greeted by salutations that announce themselves in this way: "The vision of so-and-so, which he saw concerning Judah and Jerusalem, in the days of this-and-that king of Judah."

Almost every prophetic book of the Old and New Testaments is a written account of a dream or a vision. The prophets were dreamers. They were seers. They were men and women who believed in signs. They were generally directed and controlled by the Spirit. The Spirit himself was the active element in and through all these

42

manifestations, without whom they would have been impossible. This is why God, desirous of expanding the scope of endowment and manifestation above and beyond the inner circle of His choice servants, decided to effect an outpouring of the Holy Ghost upon all flesh, so that sons and daughters would prophesy; young men would see visions, and old men would dream dreams. There is absolutely no way to separate dreams and visions from Christianity, and still have Christianity. You will end up with something else.

THE PLACE OF DREAMS IN PUBLIC LIFE

One of the interesting things about God is that He is just as interested in the affairs of the ungodly as He is in the affairs of his own people, for different reasons; He does not administer the same grace to the one that He does to the other. But He is nonetheless interested. In many cases the administration of God's grace to the ungodly is determined by the way in which such a situation will affect His people. He administers and He advises. We will discover God's hand very much at work in the public arena

In practice, we will find God actively directing the affairs of men and women in public life through the agency of dreams and visions. There is no sphere of activity excluded from this influence. God does speak and guide the affairs of persons not directly connected with his Kingdom.

In Genesis chapter 41, there is the story of Pharaoh's

dream in which God sought to warn him of the impending danger of acute famine.

> "And it came to pass at the end of two full years, that Pharaoh dreamed and, behold, he stood by the river. And behold, there came up out of the river seven well-favored kine and fat fleshed; and they fed in a meadow. And behold, seven other kine came up after them out of the river, ill favored and lean-fleshed; and stood by the other kine upon the brink of the river. And the ill favored and lean fleshed kine did eat up the seven well-favored and fat kine. So Pharaoh awoke: And he slept and dreamed the second time: and, behold, seven ears of corn came up upon one stalk, rank and good. And, behold, seven thin ears and blasted with the east wind sprung up after them. And the seven thin ears devoured the seven rank and full ears. And Pharaoh awoke, and, behold, it was a dream. And it came to pass in the morning that his spirit was troubled; and he sent and called for all the magicians of Egypt, and all the wise men thereof: and Pharaoh told them his dream, but there was none that could interpret them unto Pharaoh." (Genesis 41:1-8)

This is a classic example of a very urgent message communicated through dreams. Two startling dreams in one night speak of a message with a specific urgency, and

Pharaoh sensed within himself that something was amiss.

Notice again that the recipient of these dreams was a heathen, whilst the dreams themselves came from God; they didn't come from Pharaoh's gods because neither could the magicians nor any of the priests of Pharaoh proffer an interpretation of Pharaoh's dreams. Not until Joseph, a prophet of the most- high God, was summoned would an interpretation be given and a solution found to what should have been a national and regional disaster.

Like we pointed out in the previous chapter when we considered the allegory of Nebuchadnezzar's court, there is a divine gift of dreams, visions and their interpretation that ranks higher than any mystical or occult media in terms of possessing the purity and purpose of the Divine wisdom. God can, and does, administer this resource freely among, not only His own, but also individuals in public arena.

Again, in Daniel 2:1 we see another example of God's administration of dreams in the public sphere.

> "And in the second year of the reign of Nebuchadnezzar, Nebuchadnezzar dreamed dreams, wherewith his spirit was troubled, and his sleep brake from him."

We know the famous dream of the historic image of gold, silver, brass, and iron. Again, the college of mystics was assembled, but to no avail. Not until Daniel was found could an interpretation be proffered. God again sought to administer guidance and health to a heathen government through a dream.

Another case showing God's guiding grace in the arena of public life can be seen in prophecy predicting the destruction of the Egyptian kingdom when they fell into the hands of the king of Babylon. God said their fall would be so great they would never again rise to a position of prominence among the nations, a situation that is evident today. Most importantly, God said before this terrible event occurred He would "cover the heavens so that the stars do not shine", in the sense that the free graces of guidance by dreams, visions, portents, and other media, would be withdrawn with the result that no one, from the least to the greatest in the Egyptian kingdom, would have any premonition or warning of the impending invasion by Babylon's forces. This prophecy is found in Ezekiel 32:1-8, and is couched in very symbolic language that can be a little confusing, but the meaning will be evident from the context.

> "And it came to pass in the twelfth year, in the first day of the month, that the word of the Lord came unto me, saying, Son of man, take up a lamentation for Pharaoh, King of Egypt, and say unto him, Thou art like a young lion of the nations, and Thou art as a whale in the seas: and thou camest forth with thy rivers, and troublest the waters with thy feet, and fouledst their rivers. Thus saith the Lord God; I will therefore

spread out my net over thee with a company of people; and they shall bring thee up in my net. Then will I leave thee upon the land, I will cast thee forth upon the open field, and will cause all the fouls of the heaven to remain upon thee, and I will fill the beasts of the whole earth with thee. And I will lay thy flesh upon the mountains, and fill the valleys with thy height. I will also water with thy blood the land wherein thou swimmest, even to the mountains; and the rivers shall be full of thee. And when I shall put thee out, I will cover the heaven, and make the stars thereof dark; I will cover the sun with a cloud, and the moon shall not give her light. All the bright lights of heaven will I make dark over thee, and set darkness upon thy land, saith the Lord God."

I am sure you can see from the context (and if you read down to the end of that chapter the explanation will be given) that the "whale" drawn out of the seas to the dry land where it is devoured by the birds of prey and the wild beasts speaks of proud Egypt being lured out to battle against a company of armies mightier than she. The heavens covered so that the stars, the sun, and moon, are dark and do not give their light speak of the free and spontaneous graces of divine guidance through dreams, visions, portents, and omens being withdrawn so that the entire nation, its counselors, and princes are left in the dark about an imminent danger they should otherwise have been prepared for.

This was the case then, and it is the same today where God's grace is administered to both the godly and ungodly through guidance by dreams, and by visions. Whether man hearkens or recognizes that guidance is another matter. But it is administered just the same.

THREE KINDS OF DREAMS

Let us now proceed into an examination of three different kinds of dreams.

1.NIGHTMARES - Punishment

I am sure we are all familiar with what a nightmare is. Most of us have had a nightmare at one time or another. Generally, we find that this is a particular experience we do not wish to be repeated as it oftentimes occasions very frightful, and seriously depressing circumstances. The popular film series *A Nightmare on Elm Street* provides very vivid and graphic insight into the nature and effect of nightmares on people. In this film series an admixture of events leading to the death of a seriously deranged and demon-possessed killer results in his murderous spirit stalking, menacing, and harassing a series of unsuspecting youths through dreams (the parents of the youths shared culpability in the death of the killer).

From our illustration above, you have probably deduced that the general character of such dreams can be defined in a single word: punishment. Nightmares are generally designed to exact harrowing mental, psychological, and at times physical, circumstances upon the victims concerned. Punishment may come from the devil as a result of some form of satanic oppression, as in the case mentioned above, or it may come from God as resultant retribution or effect of actions we may or may not have taken.

I have heard testimony from brethren whom God desired to use for His work having related encounters. In one case, this young man had received the call of God into prophetic ministry and sought to flee from it. He gained employment as a clerical staff of one of the multinational oil companies based in the Nigerian Delta region. After a few weeks, his British supervisor called him one morning and told him that while he could not explain it, he had the most distressing dream the previous night in which he suffered terrible afflictions from persons who told him he must release the brother from his employ or suffer dire consequences. He persuaded the brother to go with a full month's wages.

In another case, a young man who was, as yet, unaware of the call of God on is life, secured employment in a bank. After a fortnight, his boss summoned him and told him that for several days he had been severely beaten in a dream on account of this brother being in his employ. He gave this brother a full month's wages, and begged him to go as far away from him as possible. Both these accounts are examples of the punishment one receives through nightmares.

A similar case can also be found in the gospels where Pilate's wife came to him and persuaded him to have nothing to do with the trial of Jesus because of distressing dreams she had about him. (Matthew 27:7-19)

> "Therefore when they were gathered together, Pilate said unto them, whom will ye that I release unto you? Barabbas, or Jesus which is called Christ? For he knew that for envy they had delivered him. When he was set down on the judgment seat, his wife sent unto him, saying, Have thou nothing to do with that just man: for I have suffered many things this day in a dream because of him."

Other cases might not be so straightforward. There are complicated cases of satanic oppression that lead to very upsetting and sometimes fatal nightmares. Cases of people being pursued by unknown persons in their dreams night after night are very common. I know of a woman who had a child possessed of an evil spirit. Whenever she spanked the child for being naughty or disobedient she would dream at night of the child strangely overpowering her and beating her mercilessly. It was no joking matter as she would awake each time seriously ill after the beating she received in her dreams. I have come across these and other like cases often, and I found that they generally bring very unpleasant punishment to the victims.

Job complains of like ailments in the time of his oppression.

"When I say, my bed shall comfort me, my couch shall ease my complaint; Then thou scarest me with dreams, and terrifiest me through visions: so that my soul chooseth strangling, and death rather than my life. I loathe it; I would not live alway: let me alone; for my days are vanity." (Job 7:13-16)

I am sure there are many other cases, all of them equally unpleasant. These are all nightmares and they signify to the victim that he or she is seriously oppressed and in need of deliverance.

2. RESTLESS DREAMS - Star Trek

The motion picture adaptation of the legendary television series *Star Trek* I have used to illustrate this concept of restless dreams. "To roam the stars; to go where no one has ever gone before." This theme forms a descriptive backdrop or canvas over which one can frame dreams of this category.

Basically, restless dreams are the result of strenuous mental exercise before, or as, one goes to sleep. The spirit seems to continue the mental excursion in the ethereal state via a restless trek of sometimes- meaningless activity. Such dreams are very laborious and wearisome, and often leave one strangely worn and drained upon awaking. Many times we awake thoroughly unsatisfied with the journey we made whilst we slumbered as nothing of moment or significance happened to us.

Job has spoken aptly of these moments of restlessness.

> "So I am made to possess months of vanity, and wearisome nights are appointed to me. When I lie down, I say, when shall I arise, and the night be gone? and I am full of tossings to and fro unto the dawning of the day." (Job 7:3-4)

Throughout the multitudinous array of activities we might undertake and encounter in the course of such dreams, there may be one or two moments of light when something useful and specific happens in the course of the dream. It might just be a word suddenly spoken from unexpected quarters; or a strange intervention of aid and assistance that will bear the unmistakable stamp of divine grace. Such scant and rarefied flashes of divine providence in the course of such dreams make all the difference when we awake. In other words, don't throw a dream out the window just because it seems to have no head and no tail. Look for those subtle undertones. Somewhere you might find a direct word, statement, or action, perhaps shrouded in mystery, carrying with it a sublime message that points unmistakably to the Lord. I know that the majority of these dreams are often useless, but God can and does speak through restless dreams to reward the persistent soul with the long sought after answer.

52

I had such a dream recently. As usual, it was a seemingly meaningless soul-trek: up one hill and down another; no head and no tail. I eventually became wearied during the course of the dream when all of a sudden a familiar friend stepped out of an alley and told me his wife had just died. I was dumbstruck and fumbled, trying to offer some feeble consolation. From that point onward, the dream continued to be a general nuisance until I awoke.

Because of my experience in such dreams I knew that the one thing that stood out from the entire experience was the admission from my friend about his wife's death. It was direct. I also remembered that the same friend nearly lost his wife some months ago because of a near fatal illness. It was clear the Lord was warning me to commit the woman to prayer so as to deflect whatever mischief the devil wanted to bring upon her and her family. This is one example of receiving a message through a restless dream.

There is a classic example from John's Gospel in a symbolic of the kind of experience we have just discussed.

"After these things Jesus shewed himself again to the disciples at the sea of Tiberias; and on this wise shewed he himself. There were together Simon Peter, and Thomas called Didymus, and Nathanael of Cana in Galilee, and the sons of Zebedee, and two other of his disciples. Simon Peter saith unto them, I go a fishing. They say unto him, we also go with thee. They went forth and entered into a ship immediately; and that night they caught nothing. But when the morning was now come, Jesus stood on the shore: but his disciples knew not that it was Jesus. Then Jesus saith unto them, children, have ye any meat? They answered him, No. And he said unto them, cast the net on the right side of the ship, and ye shall find. They cast therefore, and now they were not able to draw it for the multitude of fishes. Therefore that disciple whom Jesus loved saith unto Peter, it is the Lord, he girt his fishers coat unto him, (for he was naked) and did cast himself into the sea." (John 21:1-7)

Now, this is very interesting. Let us solve the riddle together.

Firstly, the theme of this passage is that Jesus showed himself (verse 1). In other words, Jesus knew he was expected to make an appearance to clarify some obscure and confusing issues. On Peter's part, his desperation was acute. To all intents and purposes, the mountain of expectations had collapsed with the crucifixion and burial of his Lord. In his perplexed and deeply confused state he went fishing, and here represents the man that falls asleep after strenuous mental exercise. The soul of the man roams and traverses the spiritual realms much the same way Peter sails the troubled waters of the night. Peter is not really looking for fish; he is trying to resolve as best he can the disappointment of his failed expectations. He is looking for the Lord. In the same way, the restless soul is trekking in search of a solution to the problem festering in its embattled mind. The Bible says "all night they caught nothing." Complete frustration awaits the like dreamer as through all his travels he comes upon no consolation. But just as dawn is breaking, between sleep and awake, the Lord himself appears and gives specific advice and instruction that satisfies the disconsolate mind. The soul, at the last minute before awaking, suddenly stumbles upon an arresting situation that provides the long sought answer.

Remember that Peter did not immediately recognize the Lord, and this squares with the problems of cognizance we suffer in the dream-state. The reason for this is that the Lord, always obliging his taste for the mysterious, will usually camouflage his appearance by adopting the general character and form of the environment of our dream-state. He will draw you out as to your inner mind. He asked Peter's company this question: "Children, have ye any meat?" Of course he knew they hadn't, and they replied telling Him same. Then came the message, the consolation and the recognition. I hope you have grasped the mystery behind that passage of scripture.

3. VISIONS - Special Delivery Service

These kinds of dreams are just that -- visions. There is urgency; there are arresting circumstances; everything associated with a special delivery mail service. Steps are taken to ensure your full attention is secured.

These dreams are not usually as long and drawn out as nightmares and restless dreams, although they could be. Sometimes they come after a nighttime of dreaming, just before -- or as -- day is breaking; when you are between sleep and awake. At such times, the spirit is still very alert and attuned to the spiritual realm, and so though you may in fact be awake, direct messages frequent themselves during this period. Many times in the fade out of such a vision I find that I am actually awake, whilst I thought myself to be asleep.

Remember that in the symbolic passage of John 21:1-7 it was as morning broke that the vision of Jesus appeared to Peter after a nighttime of soul trekking. This is the period when such visions occur.

There are other times when such dreams that are actually visions occur. Remember that the singular feature of such visions is that they are direct, and have a specific message. They leap out at you and trigger involuntary muscular or other bodily reaction -- the way 3D characters and imagery seem to leap out at you in a 3D or IMAX movie theater. They do not equivocate. These are direct messages from God. Other times when such visions happen are at night, and you wake up immediately they happen. It is as if the vision itself drags you out of sleep so that you are awake when it happens and left alone to contemplate and meditate on its meaning.

I know there will be unusual and exceptional cases of dreaming that may include all three aspects of dreaming as well as others that I have not mentioned. But I think that basically they can be arranged into these three broad groups.

THREE STAGES OF THE GIFT OF DREAMS

There are three different stages or levels of dreaming. Most dreamers in the secular and Christian spheres may experience more of the first stage of dreaming, although even this stage is a rarefied experience among people who have not yet matured spiritually. More spiritually mature believers will experience more of the second stage. The third stage is a degree of dreaming common to the most developed dreamers and seers. This degree of dreaming belongs properly to people who have the gift of prophecy, or are prophets. In fact, such people will experience a collection of all three levels of dreaming combined. These are real dreamers. Let us now consider what these stages or degrees are by examining yet another symbolic passage of scripture in John's Gospel.

> "The first day of the week cometh Mary Magdalene early, when it was yet dark, unto the sepulchre, and seeth the stone taken away from the sepulchre. Then she runneth, and cometh to Simon Peter, and to the other disciple, whom Jesus loved, and saith unto them, They have taken away the Lord out of the sepulchre, and we know not where they have laid him. Peter therefore

went forth, and that other disciple, and came to the sepulchre. So they ran both together: and the other disciple did outrun Peter, and came first to the sepulchre. And he stooping down, and looking in, saw the linen clothes lying; yet went he not in. Then cometh Simon Peter following him, and went into the sepulchre, and seeth the linen clothes lie, And the napkin, that was about his head, not lying with the linen clothes, but wrapped together in a place by itself." (John 20:1-7)

I wonder if you have noted the general theme of this passage. Yes, it is *seeing*. Each one of the three persons that went into the sepulcher (Mary, Peter, and John) saw something different, because each successive person went deeper than the other. This is the way it is with dreamers and seers.

In the first stage, Mary came to the sepulcher and saw the stone taken away from the sepulcher. She is our first dreamer, and this is the extent of her dream before she awakens. What she saw could have any number of explanations, but since her dream was not explicit she is confused. Hear her hysterical complaint to her brethren: "They have taken away the Lord out of the sepulcher, and we know not where they have laid him."

Such dreams just present a situation without giving you a clue as to the mystery behind it, as to cogent reasons, causes, and solutions. Remember that dreams, visions, prophecies, etc., are all about unraveling mysteries, solving problems, shedding light where there is darkness.

A lady who was spiritually oppressed and hindered in the area of childbirth, dreamed of herself trying to harvest ears of corn. In her dream, she would find herself either plucking corn that turned out to be unhealthy from the farm, or trying unsuccessfully to harvest such corn. Sometimes she would go to the market in her dreams to buy corn, but on arrival back home she would discover that what she had procured was very unsatisfactory for her use. All these dreams would correspond with the time of dashed hopes when she had expected to conceive.

This is a classic case of the first stage of dreaming that does not proffer anything beyond a brief snapshot of the overall situation leaving you in the dark as to important details. This stage of dreaming is the most common, and most dreamers in the secular and religious spheres dream dreams of this sort.

In the second stage, we see that John came to the sepulcher, observed all that had been told him, and then stooped down to peer in deeper for a better view of the situation. He saw other things that Mary did not see because she could not see as deeply. John saw the linen clothes lying -- a related situation.

Dreamers of this second sort can see a bit deeper, in terms of appraising more evenly a situation as to causal factors. In the case of the troubled sister I used in my previous example, after much fasting and prayer, whenever she dreamed of her problem she would no longer see this first case of trying to harvest corn, she would now see a woman (whom she knew) coming to struggle with her and deal blows to her belly. These graphic dreams would correspond with her disappointment. The case of the spiritual intruder (a witch) who was well known to her was also confirmed by other prophets, and prayers were offered in a more direct and specific manner because a case had now been established as to causal factors.

Another person, say, a brother, may dream of losing his job. (1st stage) He (or someone spiritually higher) may even dream of a misunderstanding that leads to this dismissal. (2nd stage) These are both different levels of dreaming. The third stage goes into the in-depth examination of the situation and may provide many useful answers.

In the third stage, Peter comes to the sepulcher, but he not only stoops down; he enters into the sepulcher, and is able to studiously examine all the factors and clues related to the solving of the mystery. He sees everything the other two have seen and something extra: he sees the head napkin not lying carelessly with the other linen clothes, but folded neatly in a place together by itself. If, indeed, our Lord's body was stolen the thieves would not have carefully folded the headdress, but would have left it lying carelessly with the other grave clothes in their haste to make good their escape.

So, we see that the third degree of dreamers have the grace to the extent that they can enter deep into the spiritual realm and take the time to examine clues relative to the solving of the mystery. This is a case of deep trance or vision where one can examine the details of a situation.

Upon meeting the sister I have previously spoken about and hearing her story, I was troubled as to why that situation should persist even after revelation of the identity of the intruder and different prayers had been offered. One night I dreamed. In my dream I saw the sister concerned feeling, as she was, troubled by her predicament. I began to see how she would receive and attend special prayers after special prayers for deliverance. I saw that upon her return home, she would be visited in the nighttime in her own dreams by this intruder who would hypnotize her by speaking to her in a strange language, and then interview her concerning her activities for the day. If she had received prayers and spiritual attention anywhere she would be forced to say so and reveal the line of prayer. The intruder would then take this information and counter whatever progress had been made in this sister's condition, so that the problem continued to persist.

When I saw all this, an angel of God in my dream told me that this has been the mysterious problem but there was one more thing the Lord would do, and the problem would never re-occur. I told the sister my dream, and it was the beginning of a new battle from that day onward. This is a case of advanced level dreaming.

Frequently I have entered into dreams possessed of an uncanny ability to remain in the dream state long enough to survey, study, and examine detailed material relative to events, persons, and issues.

In the case of the dreams of the man who lost his job, an advanced level dreamer would not only see the misunderstanding, but he would presently watch the scene unfolding, and perhaps, follow one or two persons from that spot to another clandestine meeting place where, unnoticed, he would eavesdrop and gather useful information bearing on the actual reasons for the dismissal.

There are other prophets of a considerably higher level who can go into trance during prayer. These people enter the vision and remain in it for several minutes, investigating, searching, studying and examining, and by the time they come out of it they are able to provide solutions to otherwise difficult problems. But even among this sort, there are different degrees of seeing and some can see farther than others. I have had meaningful associations with many of such prophets.

For two examples of this sort of trance vision, examine first Ezekiel 8:1-18 where we see that after pulling Ezekiel into the realm from his conscious prayerful state, the Lord takes him through a step by step examination of factors relating to Israel's apostasy. After each stage, the Lord instructs Ezekiel to "turn again, and I will show you greater things than these..." and then He takes Ezekiel deeper into the vision (the phrase "turn again" is an injunction compelling the man of God to sanctify himself further -- pray, worship, meditate, focus, etc. so that a deeper secret or degree of the revelation might be opened up to him).

The second example is the book of Revelation by the apostle John, which is a collection of such cases of in-depth trance vision. This is one of the higher levels of prophecy.

> "And he said, hear now my words: if there be a prophet among you, I the Lord will make myself known unto him in a vision, and will speak unto him in a dream." (Numbers 12:6)

Chapter Three

The Uncertain Sound

In this chapter, we shall be dealing with the interpretation of dreams and visions; understanding dreams and visions. I think this is a most crucial subject and relevant to our daily devotions. In 2 Corinthians 14:7-11, the apostle Paul makes a statement bearing on this subject.

> "And even things without life giving sound, whether pipe or harp, except they give a distinction in the sounds, how shall it be known what is piped or harped? For if the trumpet give an uncertain sound, who shall prepare himself to the battle?...There are, it may be, so many kinds of voices in the world, and none of them is without signification. Therefore, if I know not the meaning of the voice, I shall be unto him that speaketh a barbarian, and he that speaketh shall be a barbarian to me."

I would like to dwell on two statements from that passage of scripture. "If the trumpet give an uncertain sound who shall prepare himself to the battle?" and "There are so many kinds of voices (sounds) in the world, and none of them is without signification" (i.e., without meaning).

The above two statements are keys to this chapter. Every message has its own meaning, and if the meaning is not known the message will be misunderstood, and worst of all may go unheeded.

This matter of the interpretation of dreams and visions is no light matter. I suppose that most people have had difficulty in understanding the myriad dreams they have had. This is not strange, and so we will take our time to consider...

SOME COMMON CONCEPTS AND BASIC PRINCIPLES

1. ALERTNESS AND ATTENTIVENESS

Many times we seem to experience more apparently useless and meaningless dreams than useful and important ones. This may not actually be the case. God may be sending us many more signals and messages than we realize, but we discard most of our dreams because they are hard to understand. Sometimes dreams are hard to understand because we are not attentive and spiritually alert enough to sufficiently observe the unfolding of the dream and so have a good understanding of it. There are three reasons for a lack of spiritual alertness, but before we consider these let us research this matter of alertness a little further.

"In the visions of God brought he me into

the land of Israel, and set me upon a very high mountain, by which was as the frame of a city on the South. And he brought me thither, and, behold, there was a man, whose appearance was like the appearance of brass, with a line of flax in his hand and a measuring reed; and he stood in the gate. And the man said unto me, son of man, behold with thine eyes, and hear with thine ears, and set thine heart upon all that I shall shew thee; for to the intent that I might shew them unto thee art thou brought hither: declare all that thou seest to the house of Israel" (Ezekiel 40:2-4).

Now, the city set on a mountain is the message the Lord has sent to Ezekiel. The man in the gate is the angelic spirit assigned to explain the vision or dream to him. Note that before commencing the message the spirit guide enjoins Ezekiel to "behold with thine eyes, and hear with thine ears, and set thine heart upon all that I shall shew thee; for to the intent that I might shew them unto thee art thou brought hither: declare all that thou seest to the house of Israel." In other words, he asks for Ezekiel's undivided attention. He attempts to secure Ezekiel's interest in the matter. If he does not or cannot achieve this, the object for which he has brought Ezekiel here will be defeated, because then Ezekiel will not grasp fully the gist of the message and will be unable to deliver same to the people.

This is the problem of many prophets and servants of

the Lord in today's flashy and glamorous world. Their hearts are set on earthly things. They have not given the Lord their undivided attention. Consequently, when the Spirit comes to guide them they do not accurately grasp the gist of the message, and end up delivering a patchwork message to the sheep. This is one of the reasons why the Christian church worldwide is in such a terrible state of confusion today.

Spiritual things require avid attention and focus. If the heart is not basically interested or is by and large distracted, there will be chaos due to a misrepresentation of God's counsel. Similarly, avowed Christian faithful in general fail to receive counsel from the Lord through these media because of a divided heart; a heart set on carnal things and that cannot understudy the Spirit of God. In this case, whatever they receive from the Lord will go unheeded, because though they see with their eyes, they will not perceive, and though they hear with their ears they will not understand. They are spiritual strangers to God.

Matthew, in his Gospel, reiterates a prophecy by Isaiah about moral conditions that obtained in his time, which obtained in the time of the gospels, and are still obtainable today among people of God.

"Therefore speak I unto them in parables: because they seeing see not; and hearing they hear not, neither do they understand. And in them is fulfilled the prophecy of Esaias, which saith, By hearing ye shall hear, and shall not understand; and seeing ye shall see, and shall not perceive: for this people's heart is waxed gross, and their ears are dull of hearing, and their eyes have they closed; lest at any time they should see with their eyes, and hear with their ears, and should understand with their heart, and should be converted, and I should heal them."

(Matthew 13:13-15)

The greatest problem of Christians in not understanding their dreams, as well as the widespread misrepresentation and decline in preaching and teaching by ministers, rests on this matter of having a divided heart. They cannot hear from God. And where they still hear, it is of no use because they cannot understand what they hear. In fact, the problem is so pronounced today that you will find Christians resignedly referring to these media of divine communication as satanic, or having expired with the close of the apostolic dispensation. This foolishness is the result of a falling away from deep fellowship with, and devotion to the Lord.

We have an explosion of "born-again" Christianity; we have the flamboyance of televangelism and the advent of the mega-church industry. But do we have an abundance of true followers, disciples and ministers of our Lord? Do we have an abundance of people who stand before the Lord in fellowship day and night? Where they may be found they are few in number, and mostly few in strength. They are the remnant of what in the beginning at Pentecost started as a dynamic spiritual expansion of the true house of God.

The culture of worldliness has crept into the church so that today it is hard to distinguish between the two. Even in the midst of avowed spiritual groups we see the world, and its gods, firmly entrenched and venerated, so that this problem of a lack of understanding of spiritual things becomes more a problem of a counter-orientation away from the things of the Spirit, and towards the things of the world. The result is that try as we might under the present circumstances, we cannot comprehend the things of the Spirit of God -- "By hearing ye shall hear, and shall not understand; and seeing ye shall see, and shall not perceive: for this people's heart is waxed gross, and their ears are dull of hearing, and their eyes have they closed; lest at any time they should see with their eyes, and hear with their ears, and should understand with their heart, and should be converted, and I should heal them." (Matthew 13:13-15)

Paul addresses this matter from another perspective in Romans 8:4-7, 14 where he stipulates that a practical union and orientation with the Spirit of God is the distinguishing mark and factor of true sonship:

> "That the righteousness of the law might be fulfilled in us, who walk not after the flesh, but after the Spirit. For they that are after the flesh do mind the things of the flesh; but they that are after the Spirit the things of the Spirit. For to be carnally minded is death; but to be spiritually

minded is life and peace. Because the carnal mind is enmity against God: for it is not subject to the law of God, neither indeed can be. So then they that are in the flesh cannot please God...For as many as are led by the Spirit of God, they are the sons of God."

The big lesson here is the love of the world that is in us. If we do not reduce this love significantly and ultimately do away with it, we will not be equipped with the correct spiritual orientation to properly comprehend the mysteries of God. The voice of the Spirit, the message of the Spirit, and the leading of the Spirit will be lost on us because of the dulling effect the love for the world will have on our spiritual senses.

> "Love not the world, neither the things that are in the world. If any man love the world, the love of the Father is not in him. For all that is in the world, the lust of the flesh, and the lust of the eyes, and the pride of life, is not of the Father, but is of the world. And the world passeth away, and the lust thereof: but he that doeth the will of God abideth forever." (1 John 2:15-17)

Another reason for lack of spiritual alertness in revelation is the concept of spiritual maturity. For some Christians, not being sufficiently developed spiritually often leads to an inability to grasp and appreciate the significance of spiritual experiences. We have an example in Matthew 17:1-7.

"And after six days Jesus taketh Peter, James, and John his brother, and bringeth them up into an high mountain apart, And was transfigured before them: and his face did shine as the sun, and his raiment was white as the light. And behold, there appeared unto them Moses and Elias talking with him. Then answered Peter, and said unto Jesus, Lord, it is good for us to be here: if thou wilt, let us make here three tabernacles; one for thee, and one for Moses and one for Elias. While he yet spake, behold, a bright cloud overshadowed them: and a voice out of the cloud, which said, This is my beloved Son, in whom I am well pleased; hear ye him, And when the disciples heard it, they fell on their face, and were sore afraid. And Jesus came and touched them, and said, Arise, and be not afraid."

In this vision, we see that because of spiritual immaturity Peter ventured to put a wrong construction on the meaning and purpose of the vision of Christ's transfiguration. It was the intervention of God by his Voice from the bright cloud that silenced Peter and allowed for counsel to be concluded between Jesus, Moses and Elijah.

At other times, we might find Christians put off or discouraged because they had an encounter that went beyond their spiritual capacity. This is not out of order. God frequently takes us from one spiritual level to another by introducing us, from time to time, to experiences above our level. These things condition us for higher spiritual activity. The times that I have had experiences that left me totally baffled and upset have usually been signals that something great and arresting was awaiting me in the near future. I just had to wait until the time for appropriation came.

The third and final reason for lack of alertness is inordinate affections. By this I mean a distracting affection that hinders one from getting an accurate picture of things. Let us take an example from Revelation 17:3-7.

> "So he carried me away in the spirit into the wilderness: and I saw a woman sit upon a scarlet colored beast, full of names of blasphemy, having seven heads and ten horns. And the woman was arrayed in purple and scarlet color, and decked with gold and precious stones and pearls, having a golden cup in her hand full of abominations and filthiness of her fornication. And upon her forehead was a name written, MYSTERY, BABYLON THE GREAT, THE MOTHER OF HARLOTS AND ABOMINATIONS OF THE EARTH. And I saw the woman drunken with the blood of the martyrs of Jesus: and when I saw her, I wondered with great admiration. And the angel said unto me, wherefore didst thou marvel? (a stern rebuke) I will tell thee the mystery of the woman, and of the beast that carrieth her, which hath the seven heads and ten horns."

Observe that John, in the vision, had an inordinate affection for the beautiful and magnificently attired woman straddled upon the monstrous beast. This is not strange if you can imagine the way it all appeared in the vision: a blend of magnificent wealth and riches with a forcefully alluring and seductive feminine feature atop a beast that exudes absolute power and authority. This is what John saw, and it nearly swept him off his feet as to an inaccurate impression of its meaning if not for the spiritual guide's stern rebuke. The angel shook him back to his senses and began to expose the subterfuge and hypocrisy of the main character in the vision. At times, we might find ourselves similarly impressed by a distracting feature in our dream that will damage completely our understanding of the dream, and its message.

Conversely, many times we awake from a dream to discover we remember very little, if any of it and this is sometimes due to the fact that the dream or its subject did not really interest us, and so our spirit was decidedly inattentive to whatever transpired in the dream. This happens especially at times when we have been anxious about a particular counsel, reply, or advice, from the Lord, and our desperation is such that anything else we receive not bearing directly on our expectation we ignore. Consequently, we will find upon awaking that although we dreamed clearly we retained little substance from the dream. This is all about the matter of attentiveness and alertness.

2. DREAMS GENERALLY ASSUME THE FORM, SHAPE AND CONTEXT OF OUR FAMILIAR SOCIAL AND HISTORICAL ENVIRONMENT.

Remember the symbolic passage from John 21:1-7? Let us take a look at verses 4-7 again.

> "But when the morning was now come, Jesus stood on the shore: but the disciples knew not that it was Jesus. Then Jesus saith unto them, children, have ye any meat? They answered him, No. And he said unto them, cast the net on the right side of the ship, and ye shall find. They cast therefore, and now they were not able to draw it for the multitude of fishes. Therefore that disciple whom Jesus loved saith unto Peter, It is the Lord."

Notice that the disciples did not immediately recognize Jesus, nor did they fully understand what was happening when this apparent stranger began to make conversation with them and issue instructions. This is the way it is with some of our dreams. They do not seem plausible. They do not appear garbed in robes of plausibility.

When God sometimes wants to speak and commune with us He doesn't come through the front door as we would expect a normal visitor to do. He may come in through the back door or through the window. It was when they complied with the directives issued by Jesus and saw the fantastic results that it became clear to the disciples this elaborate drama depicted a scene that was true of the Lord. It was in keeping with his character to perform the miraculous feat of an enormous catch of fish. He had done this thing before (see Luke 5:1-10) and they remembered. It was at this point that one of them remarked: "It is the Lord" (verse 7). At this point there was an understanding of the revelation. In the same way, until we take a second look at what may at once appear to be fantastic nonsense we may not have the understanding of our dream and things may not be clear and concise.

Many times we may have dreams, sometimes recurrent, as God tries to get across a particular message to us. Such dreams may depict familiar scenes from our childhood or school days which taken together we might find rather cumbersome to contemplate. The Lord and His message may appear garbed in these robes of our familiar socio-spiritual environment. A closer look at such dreams will uncover the underlining wisdom of the communication we have received from God.

Personally, I would from time to time have dreams that projected and displayed familiar elements from my childhood. We had a large farm behind our house in Zaria, in northern Nigeria where I spent part of my childhood days. On this farm grew nearly every common Nigerian vegetable you can think of. We also grew corn, yams, and groundnuts. I remember going out to the farm in the afternoons after school to play and wander in the marvelous green jungle that was behind our house.

I remember watching the corn shoots as they grew and ripened unto harvest. I also remember the times we would harvest tomatoes, peppers, sweet potatoes, and yams. These were all precious moments of my childhood days. Much later in life, and since residing in different places at different times, I have had recurrent dreams at different periods depicting the scenery of our farm many years ago. Sometimes I would see the corn crop as it was in those days, but it would be fairly young and tender shoots a few inches from the ground. At other times, I would see the corn crop almost full-grown and bearing ears of corn. These dreams God gave to show me different periods of grace and blessing in my life. In the one instance, when the shoots were still tender and young, I was expected to exercise patience with prayers so that the promises of God in my life would not tarry too long before fulfillment. In other instances, when the proud stalks bore ears of corn, I was being made to understand that the long awaited blessings were about to manifest. God gave me guidance, advice, and encouragement through these dreams.

A sister will speak of dreams that bring to mind very vivid pictures of a childhood home with the comforts and security of family, friends, and loved ones. In her dreams, whenever enemies are pursuing her she would run and hide in her childhood home appearing once again as a little child, and protected and reassured by her parents and family. Such dreams were given her by the Lord to assure her of His protection and care in moments of particular spiritual crisis and trials.

Another typical example of such dreams can be found in the story of a man who in his college days had a very unpleasant and unfortunate experience. As a young man in school who was very interested in sports he won the respect and confidence of his games master to the extent that he was put in charge of the games room that housed all the sports equipment and paraphernalia. In what he considered a situation of desperate need, he acted against his better judgment and pawned off some equipment that was in his care thinking it would not be missed. But to his surprise, it was at this time the games master decided to take inventory of the equipment and the discrepancy was discovered.

Our friend was unable to account for the equipment he had sold and the authorities came down hard on him. He was suspended from college for two weeks and was made to pay for the stolen equipment. This experience was one of the most upsetting and disturbing of his life, and he thought he would never forget it. But he did.

Many years later, he became Chief Accounting Officer for a government department and had the charge of handling large sums of money. A personal business opportunity presented itself, and he used office funds that were in his possession hoping to replace them once the business was concluded.

All seemed well, until one night he had a dream. He saw himself back in college and the familiar scenes and drama of what was, until that time, the most disturbing experience of his life were played back and culminated in his being disgraced publicly at the announcement of his suspension. He awoke from this terrifying dream with a start, beads of sweat spread across his forehead. After anxious moments of serious contemplation, he perceived that a warning was being sounded about his misappropriation of office funds. He immediately made haste to refund the office funds from other sources without waiting for the business deal to be concluded.

A few days later, he had cause to thank God for His timely warning and rebuke: A surprise visit by auditors was made to his department, and all accounts were audited. By the grace of God through a strange dream a very sad and disastrous situation was avoided.

Again, there is the story of a woman who frequently dreamed of playing in the stream with childhood friends. From her youth, these dreams of appearing as a child, playing, and bathing with childhood friends in the stream were very common. She took it for granted that they were just funnily interesting dreams with no meaning since she saw herself as a child again playing with familiar friends. As God would have it, she came to know the Lord, and became devoted in His service.

Much later, she again had this funny dream. But this time, as the other children called out to her to join them in the stream, a stern-faced stranger appeared and warned her not to continue participating in those games. He further enjoined her not to enter the stream anymore. She told this dream and the others to her Pastor, who explained that from her childhood she had been oppressed by water-spirits (*mamy wata* or mermaids in West African lore). He explained further that since she had come to know the Lord there had been a process of deliverance from these influences. We see again how the spiritual conditions of the dream-state are blended in with the familiar socio-spiritual environment of the dreamer.

3. DREAMS AS AGENTS OF SPIRITUAL OPPRESSION.

This concept will go a long way to serve as a key to unlock the mystery behind the myriad dreams and related experiences that frequent our spiritual horizons.

In the matter of spiritual oppression dreams have played, and do play, a classic role in facilitating the processes that lead to different degrees of satanic oppression and affliction in the lives of people in both public and church life. One major factor employed by evil forces to introduce spiritual corruption in the dream state that is designed to have corresponding negative and destructive influences on the physical well-being of persons in their waking state is the factor of eating in dreams.

From a purely West African context (which will have its parallels to a greater or lesser degree in the cultures of other regions), poisons of different kinds have traditionally been administered through foods and drinks. When I speak of poisons, I refer not only to fatal poisons, but poisons of different kinds. For example, there are poisons to maim, cripple, or paralyze, all or certain parts of the body. There are poisons to retard the mental faculties, to make one lunatic. There are also poisons to retard the emotional and sentimental faculties, thereby enslaving and controlling behavioral and moral tendencies and steering people in the direction of troublesome relationships and associations. There are poisons to make one ill and sickly, and finally there are poisons that initiate a person into witchcraft. All these poisons are administered to the victims most subtly and effectively through dreams.

Between 1989 and 1990 I was poisoned twice in my dreams by a witch. I was given a strange concoction and forced to drink it. From that time I began to have a series of illnesses that the Lord later showed me ought to have killed me. But in His sovereign mercy and grace I not only survived, but early in 1994 God totally healed me.

Sometimes a person may have dreams of eating with familiars. Dreams of this kind do not always portend good. They may enslave the person to a negative situation over which he/she may have virtually no control in their conscious physical state. Such a situation could be illness, barrenness, or a purely emotional enslavement that deprives you of the will to make an independent decision apart from the influence of another. Another situation of this kind could be spiritual slumber.

Eating in dreams is also an agency by which people are initiated into witchcraft. Dreams of eating especially meats can be initiations or attempts to initiate into the occult or witchcraft. The witches prepare that food and put 'witch' into it. They then come and offer you this food in your dream. Sometimes it can be a kind of food you like very much, so that once you are presented with the food in the dream (especially by someone you know) you offer little resistance. From the time the victim has such a dream he/she will begin to see some changes in his/her life. Any time this person subsequently lays his/her head on a pillow and falls asleep they will be transported to the witch's coven and introduced to a repertoire of witching activities. Such a person may become an agent of witchcraft without even realizing it to the extent that in his/her dreams he/she may journey from place to place wreaking havoc in other people's lives. In such a situation, a normally nice person may find him/herself being possessed of a spirit of witchcraft.

One classic example of this matter of initiation and oppression by witchcraft through the agency of dreams is the case of an adult man or woman whom the witches have marked for initiation. It is generally easier to influence children than it is adults since children have a lower resistance threshold, aside from the fact that they are more easily deceived and enticed by fancies and treats. If the witches want to entrap a man or woman and/or initiate him/her into the coven, they will first of all get hold of his/her child. If it is a little girl, she will be enticed in her dream and given the food to eat. This food prepared by the witches will automatically initiate her into witchcraft, and she will become a witch. This part of it will be fairly easy. It is after this that the little girl will be sent to bring her father, or mother, as the case may be to the field of witches. He or she will begin to have strange dreams where the daughter, towards whom there will be neither skepticism, nor suspicion, will come and lead him/her to a strange place of meeting. Frequent dreams of this nature, which will be taken for granted, could lead to the adult being entrapped in one way or another, and in all probability, ultimately becoming a witch him/herself.

There are situations where a Christian who is devout in the work and service of the Lord may face such an attack by witches whereby he/she is marked for initiation. Possibly because the witch or witches in his/her family or community having observed the Christian over a period of time, and being harassed and encumbered by his/her prayers, decide that the only way to subdue the Christian spiritually is to initiate him/her into their craft. They will now begin to make advances towards the Christian in his/her dreams, and if the witch has a close relationship with the Christian there might not be too much difficulty. In fact, there might be no difficulty at all as far as giving the Christian the 'witch' to eat.

But in the case of a strong Christian, the poison may not have the desired effect. That is to say, the spirit of the Christian is too strong to be enslaved and entrapped into witchcraft, and so the Christian will be victorious to that extent. But the poison could still have other effects, possibly causing one illness or another that stubbornly resists any form of medicament until there is a spiritual deliverance through prayer.

This is a very serious and grave matter we have discussed, and I realize the potential for dispute and controversy in the claim I have made that Christians can be targeted, and eventually, enticed into witchcraft thereby losing their sanctification. I have learned this fact from experience, and there is also Biblical precedent to support this assertion.

The first, in Revelation 2:14, is an allusion to a story in the book of Numbers where the King of Moab, Balak, conspired with Balaam, a sorcerer, to entice the sanctified people of God into being joined to the children of Moab in their abominations. (See Numbers 25:1-3) Let us now take a look at Revelation 2:14.

> "But I have a few things against thee, because thou hast there them that hold the doctrine of Balaam, who taught Balac to cast a stumblingblock before the children of Israel, to eat things sacrificed unto idols, and to commit fornication."

The second, in Revelation 2:20, is an allusion to a story in the book of Kings where Jezebel, a witch, usurped the authority of the federal heads of the religious state of Israel and poisoned the people with her witchcraft (see 1 Kings16:31 & 21:25-26). Let us now look at Revelation 2:20.

> "Notwithstanding I have a few things against thee, because thou sufferest that woman Jezebel, which calleth herself a prophetess, to teach and to seduce my servants to commit fornication, and to eat things sacrificed to idols."

Brethren, let us not be ignorant of the enemy's devices. We have all heard the axiom: "what you don't know can't hurt you." This is not only untrue, it is foolish. The warning I gave earlier, was first given by the great apostle in 2 Corinthians 2:11: "Lest Satan should get an advantage of us: for we are not ignorant of his devices."

Everyone born into this world possesses a crown of grace at the instance of his/her conception. This crown of grace differs in size and glory with the individual, and symbolizes the portfolio of blessings and endowments to which the individual may aspire and achieve success. A singular aspect of these blessings is what is called the spiritual 'hedge' of protection or victory against adversaries.

In scripture, when speaking of the downfall of a man, reference is sometimes made to the spiritual hedge being taken away to allow for invasion by intruders who despoil the victim.

In Job 1:9-10, Satan, when answering the Lord's boast concerning righteous Job, refers to this protective hedge as the reason for Job's success by acting as a deterrent against satanic attack.

> "Then Satan answered the Lord, and said, Doth Job fear God for nought? Hast not thou made an hedge about him, and about his house, and about all that he hath on every side? Thou hast blessed the work of his hands, and his substance is increased in the land."

In Ecclesiastes 10:8 we are told that "he that breaketh an hedge a serpent shall bite." This refers to the misfortune to befall a man on account of satanic forces once the spiritual hedge of victory or protection is removed.

In Psalms 89:38-44, David spoke in the vision foreshadowing the suffering of Christ by the hand of Pontius Pilate and mentioned that this happened because this hedge was taken away from Christ: "Thou hast broken down all his hedges; thou hast brought his strongholds to ruin" (verse 40).

Mark 12:1 establishes conclusively the matter of this hedge of victory provided by the Lord freely to everyone who comes into the world.

"...A certain man planted a vineyard, and set an hedge about it, and digged a place for winefat, and built a tower, and let it out to husbandmen, and went into a far country."

This is the way everyone comes into this world. But sadly, they do not always remain this way. Agents of darkness work against people to break down this hedge so that their prospects and blessings are either stolen or destroyed.

Our Lord Jesus spoke of these thieves who come to steal, to kill, and to destroy, in John 10:10, all of whom represent conditions that are reflected through dreams. Dreams of going to the market to do large shopping only to be robbed on the way back home by strangers, or planting crop only to have it destroyed and devoured by wild beasts, or trying to pluck or harvest ripe corn only to be frustrated by some person or persons, and the like, are dreams that reflect this condition of the broken down hedge of victory. This victory needs to be re-established in such lives through prayer as directed by the Spirit. Such persons are usually frustrated in one way or another, and they will continue to lead miserable lives until such victory is established and the spiritual hedge rebuilt.

4. DREAMS AS AGENTS OF DIVINE GRACE.

Just as there are dreams that reflect negative conditions in our lives, there are also dreams that reflect conditions of divine grace and blessing administered from the throne of grace. Our discussion of this general concept will help in our understanding of such dreams.

There are times when we have dreams of entering some kind of conflict or struggle, and just at the point of despair a stranger comes to our aid to deliver us from our enemies to the extent that our victory, once threatened, is now re-established. Such dreams reflect a condition of victory that may apply to any one of a number of situations in which we find ourselves in our conscious physical state.

"Be not forgetful to entertain strangers: for
thereby some have entertained angels unawares."
(Hebrews 13:2)

Like we have earlier pointed out, the grace of our Lord Jesus Christ will frequently appear to us in our slumber blended in with the familiar socio-spiritual elements of our dreams. This is in keeping with what Apostle Paul has said in Hebrews 13:2 concerning our entertaining angelic visitors unawares.

Many times we entertain angelic assistance in our dreams without realizing it. The significant outplay and occurrence of help and assistance in our dreams often points to acts of deliverance by angels on our behalf that are blended in with elements of our dreams.

I remember in 1989 at a time when I received much concerted spiritual attack from the forces of darkness that the adversaries had sought to destroy me and make me useless in life. In my dream on a certain day, my body was riddled with putrefying sores from which huge maggots crawled out freely. My entire body was condemned with this maggot infestation, and as it decayed a man suddenly appeared and gave me a measure of salt asking me to rub the salt all over my decaying body. I obeyed, and immediately my body and my skin were restored clear as a newborn babe's. This is a good example of victory being won and established in a dream through the ministry of angels.

A dream like the one described above, would not mean that the victory could be taken for granted and there was no need for prayer. Such a notion would be counter-productive. The right thing to do in that kind of situation is to give myself to prayer in order to confirm and establish the victory the Lord has promised me through the dream. Such prayer, depending on the nature of my predicament, would be directed by the Spirit to establish and confirm my complete deliverance.

It is common for God to show us things in our dreams that do not materialize in the physical. Such a situation could be caused by myriad contradicting factors that may be no fault of ours. But there are also cases where we do not receive because of neglect on our part to perform the necessary processes to bring the blessing to manifestation. This is because every blessing, or grace, we receive from the Lord through dreams, visions, or any other medium must be confirmed before manifestation can be ensured. It is like endorsing a check to be redeemed for cash at a bank. I usually rebuke all negative dreams upon awaking, and confirm all positive dreams by prayer of thanks. This is a good practice.

There are also dreams where power is administered directly for deliverance from oppression, and others where power is given for service.

I have had dreams where angels have presented me with spiritual truths or prayed for me for guidance and grace in specific areas. Such dreams usually have automatic manifestation irrespective of spiritual confirmation. One would awake from his slumber in full possession of understanding and wisdom in certain spiritual matters, or the power to administer a certain grace to himself or to others.

On several occasions, I have received power in my dream to administer deliverance through prayer to a member of my family who was in danger of sudden death. God miraculously intervened to avert the disaster. On one occasion, the person had this dream in which he was instructed to seek me out to pray for him, whilst I also was similarly enjoined to stand in the gap for him because of impending danger.

Above and beyond the matter of deliverance and victory in dreams, there are cases where people have received an anointing for service through dreams.

I had a minister friend who had such experiences. Each time this minister receives an anointing from the Lord for service the experience is usually preceded by a corresponding dream depicting conferment of this power by a variety of elements. Sometimes he will see himself struggling along with others to fetch Water of Life from a Rock with an iron pail. Other times, Jesus himself would summon and give him this water to drink. And still other times he would find himself covered with snow that would eventually melt into the same Water of Life. These are all examples of dreams that administer power.

Brethren, dreams should not be taken for granted. Both arresting, and seemingly passive dreams have their significance in our lives, and we would do well to pay more attention to the administration of grace through our dreams. We should generally strive to be more spiritually alert so that regardless of the means of communication we might at least recognize the hand of God, and from hence begin to unravel the mystery behind the message. There is no form of spiritual communication that can be adequately understood without contemplation and meditation.

The nation of Israel fell to disgrace several times in Bible days and in recent history, because she did not take the time to consider the messages and utterances of the prophets.

Christendom today has lost ground spiritually, because it has neglected to consider and to contemplate the foundational apostolic principles enshrined in the New Testament Scriptures. There have been dangerous deviations and apostasies all of which appear flamboyant and glamorous to the untrained eye, but which have occasioned a situation of near-total collapse of the spiritual pillars of doctrine and practice that were originally designed to support the Christian church.

The church has lost its vision because it is no longer spiritually alert. The cares of this world have so made inroads into the fabric of Christian worship that the spiritual life of the church is being snuffed out.

We need to get back to the basics. We need to revive the vital elements of true and original Christian spirituality. That is why this book has been written, to introduce the earnest seeker to that basic spiritual faith once delivered into the safekeeping of the saints of God.

I am not naive about the dangers of writing such a book. The possibilities for misunderstanding and misrepresentation are enormous. But I have heard from the Lord on this matter, and the book must be written.

If you notice, I have deliberately shied from, and shunned, any hints of setting forth set formulas and fixed ideas about interpreting dreams. Formulas, and the like, are the work of psychics and mystics and can be misleading, unreliable, and dangerous. Interpretation of dreams and visions is a matter of understanding the ways of the Spirit of God and how He relates with the human spirit with respect to socio-spiritual development and communion. It is from this standpoint we have attempted to bring this message, based on an experimental consideration of the myriad common concepts and basic principles concerning dreams and visions, and understood and illuminated in the light of personal experience, analysis, and instruction on these matters by the Lord.

PAST, PRESENT, AND FUTURE TENSE OF SPIRITUAL REVELATION

Many times we are shown things in dream and vision that describe situations pertaining to the present time. Sometimes the time is fairly easy to determine; a number of things with which we are familiar in the dream itself might give us a clue as to its pertaining to the present.

At other times it might not be so easy to determine even with the same, or similar, highlights in the outplay of the dream whether the message relates to the present, or the future. Again, things that pertain to the future are usually displayed without much commentary apart from a casual presentation of the facts. We are left with many unanswered questions because the matter at hand pertains not to the present, but to a future period.

There are other times when we have an experience, and sometime later we see the same situation outplayed in a dream or vision. In other words, we see something that has already taken place. This may be warning to take care lest an unfortunate happening reoccur. But there are also times when this is a revelation in its past tense. This revelation could come because you had no prior notice of the physical event before it happened, and the Lord wishes to show that He had anticipated its occurrence nonetheless and had incorporated it into the scheme of things. Probably, had we been given prior notification of the event, it would have caused us much worry and disquiet, or we might not have believed it, then after the event has taken place the message now comes and is a little puzzling. Certain messages can come in the past tense.

There are certain cases where a prophet, depending on his level or degree of prophetic utterance, will speak in a vision of something that has already happened as if it were yet to come. Like I have earlier pointed out, this depends on the level or degree of prophetic utterance and vision -- the degree of development and maturity of the spirit of the prophet in communion with the Spirit of God with regard to the level of discipline and guidance the spirit of that prophet receives upon entering the vision and prophecy (the almanac). Let us pause here a moment for some scriptural confirmation of this position.

> "John to the seven churches which are in Asia: Grace be unto you, and peace, from him which is, and which was, and which is to come; and from the seven spirits which are before his throne." (Revelation 1:4)

In this salutation by the apostle, we are told that grace (i.e., the message) has been given in respect of things which are present, things which are past, and the things which are in the future. This is the nature and structure of the vision and prophecy, and revelation in general takes its character from here.

All revelation has its past, its present, and its future, tenses. The degree or level of power associated with prophetic utterance will be in accordance with the level of development and maturity of the spirit of the prophet as it relates with and is disciplined by the Spirit of God. It is the Spirit of God that takes the spirit of the prophet into vision and prophecy, and administers guidance and direction for the interpretation of the mystery by the spirit of the prophet.

> "I was in the spirit on the Lord's Day, and heard behind me a great voice, as of a trumpet, saying, I am Alpha and Omega, the first and the last: and, what thou seest, write in a book, and send it unto the seven churches..." (Revelation 1:10-11)

We have here a classic example of the nature of prophecy and prophetic utterance: the spirit of the prophet is taken into vision and prophecy by the Spirit of the Lord to be instructed and guided in the interpretation of what is seen for the benefit of God's chosen people. Our Lord's introduction of himself as "Alpha and Omega" and the "first and the last" immediately followed by the instruction on how to interpret the vision ("what thou seest, write in a book") clearly describe the system of

94

prophetic utterance. "Alpha and Omega" and "first and the last" refer to the length and breadth of Vision and Prophecy -- that scroll or screen of the heavenly mystery which the Lord stretched out and established before the foundation of the world. It is into this expansive mystery that the Lord introduces the spirit of the prophet in vision, trance, or dream.

There are times when a prophet sees a revelation in its past tense, i.e., something that has already happened is shown to him in dream or vision, and this occurs because the Spirit of the Lord wishes to use the imagery to illustrate something that pertains to the present. We see an example of this in Isaiah's vision of Lucifer's failed coup in the heaven of heavens used to illustrate the promised overthrow of the military aggression of Nebuchadnezzar of Babylon.

> "How thou art fallen from heaven, O Lucifer, son of the morning. How art thou cut down to the ground, which didst weaken the nations: For thou hast said in thine heart, I will ascend into heaven, I will exalt my throne above the stars of God: I will sit also upon the mount of the congregation in the sides of the north: I will ascend above the heights of the clouds; I will be like the most High. Yet thou shalt be brought down to hell, to the sides of the pit"

(Isaiah 14:3-23).

Reading through the entire passage indicated above in parenthesis, it is clear that the Spirit is using the imagery of Lucifer's rebellion and judgment to illustrate prophetically the destruction of proud Babylon.

Finally, let me reiterate once again that even as there are messages that have a present and a future tense, there are also revelations that come in the past tense. In the next chapter, we shall examine in detail another aspect of this matter of interpretation of mysteries by looking at a specific grace in scripture called the word of wisdom.

Chapter Four

The Word of Wisdom

We have come upon a very important subject in this matter of understanding, interpreting and generally traversing spiritually that which is hidden, secret, and mysterious. In terms of our spiritual enrichment and the ability to grasp the mysteries of God, we will demonstrate the significance of the Word of Wisdom. First, we shall introduce the concept, and then proceed to make a detailed examination of its significance in the broad sphere of Christian doctrine and practice.

THE LOST GIFT

The apostle Paul introduces this concept in his lecture on the spiritual manifestations in 1 Corinthians 12:7-8.

> "But the manifestation of the spirit is given to every man to profit withal. For to one is given by the Spirit the word of wisdom…"

Now, this wisdom gift, which can also be described as the utterance of wisdom, is an active grace that enables its possessor to search out and profess the understanding and interpretation of mysteries. We see a reference to this grace by the angel guide in John's vision of Revelation 13:18 in the form of a challenge to anyone who could translate the mysterious number of the beast into a description of the nature of the antichrist.

> "Here is wisdom. Let him that hath understanding (i.e., the interpretation of mysteries) count (i.e., effect a spiritual translation of) the number of the beast: for it is the number of a man; and his number is six hundred three score and six."

Another reference to this grace is made in Revelation 17:9 where the angel guide himself effects an interpretation of the mystery of the beautiful woman straddled upon a scarlet colored beast.

> "And here is the mind which hath wisdom. The seven heads are seven mountains on which the woman sitteth."

We see here that the wisdom gift is used in the interpretation of visions.

Daniel also possessed this gift of the utterance of wisdom. In Daniel 1:17 we are told that "God gave them (Shadrach, Mesach, and Abednego) knowledge and skill in all learning and wisdom: and Daniel had understanding in all vision and dreams."

In a graphic description of the nature of this gift the queen of Babylon, remonstrating with counselors in a near-hysterical royal court, spoke in Daniel 5:10-12.

> "Now, the queen, by reason of the words of

the king and his lords, came into the banquet house: and the queen spake and said, O King, live forever: let not thy thoughts trouble thee, nor let thy countenance be changed. There is a man in thy kingdom, in whom is the spirit of the holy gods; and in the days of thy father light and understanding and wisdom, like the wisdom of the gods, was found in him; whom the king Nebuchadnezzar thy father…made master of the magicians, astrologers, chaldeans, and soothsayers; Forasmuch as an excellent spirit, and knowledge, and understanding, interpreting of dreams, and shewing of hard sentences, and dissolving of doubts, were found in the same Daniel…"

Another well-known Bible character who possessed this grace was Joseph. We all know the story of Joseph's travails and triumphal rise to glory. He was accorded respect and recognition because of his ability to interpret dreams and visions.

In practice, there are certain people who are endowed with this grace through educated experience of dealing with the mysterious, and being inspired to be in possession of a spiritual mind. Such people have the wisdom to give interpretations to dreams, visions, and the like. There are others that would seem to be endowed with a higher aspect of this grace in the sense that when presented with a confusing and perplexing mystery by dream, or other medium, they can present a request accordingly to the Lord and receive a detailed explanation, and an unraveling of the mystery.

In the apostolic period, the fathers made use of the word of wisdom to interpret Vision and Prophecy pertaining to the Old Testament - the law and the prophets - in the light of New Testament doctrine and practice. One singular feature is the apostle Paul, who received remarkable grace to effect the most in- depth exposition of the written Old Testament mystery for the establishing of New Testament doctrine. Paul speaks of this wisdom in 1 Cor. 2:6-10.

> "Howbeit we speak wisdom among them that are perfect: yet not the wisdom of this world, nor of the princes of this world that come to nought: But we speak the wisdom of God in a mystery, even the hidden wisdom, which God ordained before the world unto our glory: which none of the princes of this world knew: for had they known it, they would not have crucified the Lord of glory. But as it is written, Eye hath not seen, nor ear heard, neither have entered into the heart of man, the things which God hath prepared for them that love him. But God hath revealed them unto us by his spirit: for the spirit searches all things, yea, the deep things of God."

Again, Peter, in his epistle speaks of the word of wisdom possessed and demonstrated by Paul in his exposition of Vision and Prophecy in the light of New

Testament doctrine.

> "And account that the long-suffering of our
> Lord is salvation; even as our beloved brother
> Paul also according to the wisdom given unto
> him hath written unto you; As in all his
> epistles, speaking in them of these things…"

Generally, the word of wisdom is concerned with the
interpretation of mysteries. We might go further to say
that this grace is, in a broader sense, associated with
appraising, appropriating, and apprehending, the
mysterious regimen of spiritual power and glory enshrined
in the fullness of the kingdom. Let us examine this
statement further by considering…

THE SIGNIFICANCE OF THE WISDOM GIFT TO THE END-TIME CHURCH

The end-time points to the attainment of full stature,
perfection, glorification, etc. – the consummation of all
things spoken before.

Peter speaks of this attainment of full stature and
perfection in 1 Peter 1:3-5.

> "Blessed be the God and father of our Lord
> Jesus Christ, which according to his abundant
> mercy hath begotten us again unto a lively hope
> by the resurrection of Jesus Christ from the
> dead, To an inheritance incorruptible, and
> undefiled, and that fadeth not away, reserved in

heaven for you, who are kept by the power of God through faith unto salvation ready to be revealed in the last time."

We are informed here of an expansive store of spiritual riches of power and glory reserved for those who will lay hold of them in the last time (the end time).

Paul, in Philippians 3:10-12 lends the weight of his personal ambition to this debate on the attainment and apprehension of the glorious store of heavenly riches reserved for the saints.

"That I may know him, and the power of his resurrection, and the fellowship of his sufferings, being made conformable unto his death, if by any means I might attain unto the resurrection of the dead. Not as though I had already attained, either were already perfect, but I follow after, if that I may apprehend that for which also I am apprehended of Christ Jesus."

We have demonstrated here an exemplary determination by the apostle to comprehend, contemplate, and appropriate by way of practical experience, the fuller riches of the glory of Christ's inheritance in the saints. In verse 15, Paul admonishes us in this way: "Let us therefore, as many as be perfect be thus minded: and if in anything ye be otherwise minded, God shall reveal even this unto you." In other words, this should be the goal of the church, and not, as is the case with some, the pursuit of worldly things.

The Christian Church ought to strive towards seizure of that heavenly cache of arms and higher capacities to demonstrate the resurrection power of Jesus Christ, making the kingdoms of this world the kingdoms of our Lord. This quest by the Christian Church is facilitated by harvesting the spiritual values inherent in the mysteries of Heaven through the word of wisdom; interpreting and unlocking spiritual mysteries and giftings of the kingdom. So that we become transformed by the measure of the revelation and our comprehension of it. Paul speaks of this process in 2 Corinthians 3:18.

> "But we all, with unveiled face, beholding as in a mirror the glory of the Lord, are being transformed into the same image from glory to glory, just as by the spirit of the Lord."

We speak here of being acquainted with the Spirit of God to an intimate degree; being able to perceive and apprehend mysteries of the heavens to the extent that we traverse the mystical corridors of the power and glories of Christ.

After the Lord displayed to Ezekiel the panoramic vision of the inheritance (for Ezekiel saw, in chapters 40 - 43, a symbolic representation of "the riches of the glory of His inheritance in the saints"), He instructed Ezekiel in this way:

> "Thou son of man, shew the house to the house of Israel, that they may be ashamed of

their iniquities: and let them measure the pattern."
(Ezekiel 43:10)

From the context of the scripture verse, to "measure the pattern" would be to consider and contemplate; to comprehend and digest. It speaks to us of appreciating the spiritual values enshrined in the mystery to such an extent that our vision, character, mentality, and entire physical life, is made to correspond with the glories of the mystery. These are elements of the word of wisdom; the grace to understand and digest mysteries of the kingdom.

Paul continually spoke of the way in which the spiritual values embedded in the mystery should affect the radiance of God's glory through us to the point where we touch the vestiges of immortality.

> "I press toward the goal for the prize of the upward call of God in Christ Jesus. Therefore let us, as many as are mature, have this mind; and if in anything you think otherwise, God will reveal even this to you. Nevertheless, to the degree that we have already attained, let us walk by the same rule, let us be of the same mind. Brethren, join in following my example, and note those who walk as you have us for a pattern." (Philippians 3:14-17)

> "For we know that if our earthly house of this tabernacle were dissolved, we have a building of God, an house not made with hands, eternal in

the heavens. For in this we groan, earnestly desiring to be clothed upon with our house which is from heaven: If so be that being clothed we shall not be found naked. For we that are in this tabernacle do groan, being burdened: not for that we would be unclothed, but clothed upon, that mortality might be swallowed up of life. Now he that hath wrought us for the selfsame thing is God, who also hath given unto us the earnest of the Spirit" (2 Corinthians 5:1-5).

Observe that the Spirit has been given to divinely establish the pedagogical system that creates in us that which grows and bears fruit unto immortality. This is an exercise wrought by the Spirit of God; a spiritual journey, a spiritual experiment.

In practice, there are experiences typical for those whom God has chosen and destined for divine service. And so it is that in many a situation in the Scriptures, these persons are given a vision of some lofty heavenly import.

In the case of Adam, he was given abundant access to that fountain of life, peace, progress, prosperity, and power, symbolized by the Tree of Life in the garden. The Garden of Eden represents the sphere of the mystical heavens which were opened to Jesus Christ at his baptism, were opened to Ezekiel in Ezekiel 1:1 and to other prophets and apostles throughout scripture. As long as Adam had access to such visions of grace characterized by the heavenly Tree, his life was known to possess a divine quality of persistent progress and power. But once he was driven from that garden, in the sense that he no longer abode in, or had access to, the fountain of grace because of sin, his life lost that quality of power, and he was reduced to the level of mere man with his share of suffering and woe.

We might say that Adam's vision of that Tree, so long as he beheld it and abode under the canopy of its grace, qualified and equipped him in a special way that was dearly missed when he fell from grace to grass. That vision qualified Adam for higher service and glory from God.

Similarly, when Moses had the strange visions on the lofty divine mountain he became empowered by the God that dwelt on that mountain. See him (Moses) possessed of such power and authority that he is able to effect that fantastic deliverance of God's people from the iron grip of Egypt's Pharaoh. See him again irradiated by that resplendent glory that shone from his face as he ministered to the people of Israel the living oracles of God. Those visions, and other experiences of glory and mystery, equipped and qualified Moses for special service.

The same could be said for Isaiah, Ezekiel, Daniel, John the Baptist, Paul, and a host of others, all of whom had a personal history recorded (and some unrecorded) to have been punctuated with these mysterious experiences that announce the equipment and ordination for special divine service.

Early in my Christian life I made spiritual journeys by divine grace into that celestial paradise where the secrets of the universe are kept; the divine reserve of riches, blessings, virtue, and grace that our Lord called "my father's house" in John 14:1-3.

> "Let not your heart be troubled; you believe in God, believe also in me. In my father's house are many mansions; if it were not so, I would have told you. I go to prepare a place for you. And if I go to prepare a place for you, I will come again and receive you unto myself; that where I am, there you may be also."

Besides the traditional interpretations of this scripture that refer to our Lord going to prepare a place in Paradise for us to enjoy after we die (we will, indeed, enjoy the blessings of that place in Paradise after we expire) the Lord was referring to the more immediate work His disciples would carry out after His decease, and how He would enter His "father's house" to obtain a special grace for each of His disciples to empower them for the special task He had ordained. Consequently, upon His death, burial, resurrection and ascension He prepared that place, and from thence sent forth the Holy Ghost to endow them from that vantage point from which He, as Lord, ruled and dominated all things.

> "But to each one of us is given grace according to the measure of the gift of Christ, Wherefore he saith, when he ascended up on

high, he led captivity captive, and gave gifts unto men...and he gave some, apostles; and some prophets; and some evangelists; and some pastors and teachers." (Ephesians 4:7, 8, 11)

As I was saying earlier, I visited this place spiritually that appeared to me in varied forms. Sometimes like a very great supermarket wherein were found all kinds of goods. There were goods for material riches and wealth, goods for healing and physical restoration of different kinds, and goods for spiritual power and grace. I went to the section for spiritual power and grace and came to the bookshelves. On one bookshelf were books on each and every angel in heaven by name, function, schedule, etc. Other stands held books of wisdom and knowledge about God's mysteries.

Each time I visited this place, I was shown a different thing. Sometimes I was shown what looked like the golden Ark of the Covenant that stood in the great and ancient temple, variously described by Old and New Testament Scriptures. All these visions, and an increasing understanding and communion with them, are designed to prepare and equip the servant of God for the special service to which he is ordained.

So it must be with the victorious church of this hour, that "he" (the "man-child") should be trained with certain lofty mystical experiences that will equip him to demonstrate the resurrection power of Jesus Christ to the world in one final manifestation of the superiority of God's kingdom.

> "And he that overcometh, and keepeth my works unto the end, to him will I give power over the nations: And he shall rule them with a rod of iron; as the vessels of a potter shall they be broken to shivers: even as I received of my father." (Revelation 2:26-27)

> "And she brought forth a man-child, who was to rule all nations with a rod of iron; and her child was caught up unto God, and to his throne." (Revelation 12:5)

As we have already pointed out, true spiritual power rests upon vision and experience, i.e., it must proceed from true empirical knowledge. There can be no power apart from this. There may be intelligence, a brilliance of sorts, even flair and charisma, but there will be no power without preparatory vision and experience. This is what makes all the difference in the service of God.

In terms of the man of God's equipment for divine service, and especially the experience and development of the man-child - that victorious company of heroic end-time saints foretold in scripture, let us examine seven steps to the fullness of the anointing of power. These seven steps are enshrined in the messages to the seven churches in Revelation 2:1 through 3:22.

Firstly, let us bear in mind that these seven "overcomeths" are prefaced with the injunction: "He that hath an ear, let him hear what the Spirit saith unto the churches." In other words, the concept of the word of wisdom - having a communion with, and an understanding of, the mysteries of God - is the guiding theme in these experiences as those with spiritual capacity are enjoined to be attentive to the Spirit of God: "He that hath an ear, let him hear what the Spirit saith."

Secondly, consider that what we are about to examine are lofty spiritual visions and experiences by which the overcomer is to be orientated by the Spirit for equipment with an anointing of power.

Some of us may have experienced things similar to what we are about to consider as to spiritual experiences in the course of our development, and we may have an idea about what they signify.

Consider that these Seven Overcomeths basically represent the Spirit's introduction of the man of God's choosing to the place of power; the place of the presence, to equip him for divine service. Upon close examination, they will be seen to further demonstrate a step by step systematic introduction to, and equipment with, the capacities and unctions for service as we proceed from vision to vision, i.e., from *overcometh* to *overcometh*, until we arrive at the seventh or final *overcometh* which, as we shall see, speaks of our having passed through every stage of development and growth until we are given a seat or chair in the very real tent (i.e. presence) of the Lord. This seat demonstrates a final appointment or placement of authority in the presence of God, in the presence of the angels, and in the presence of the saints. Let us now consider...

SEVEN STEPS TO THE FULLNESS OF SALVATION

We are faced here with the Word of God delivered under the auspices of John, the apostle. The scenario graphically presented in the vision of the Seven Overcomeths of the Revelation to John is a description of the highest level of the Word of God delivered for the instruction, development and salvation of the children of God.

An illustration of this scenario of the progressive development of salvation is found in 1 Chronicles 17: 4- 5, where King David, having expressed his desire to build an house for the Throne of the Lord, is admonished by God through Nathan, the prophet.

> "Go and tell David my servant, Thus saith the Lord, Thou shalt not build me an house to dwell in: For I have not dwelt in a house since the day that I brought up Israel unto this day; but have gone from tent to tent, and from one tabernacle to another."

Here we see the word "tabernacle" used, which can be likened to a legislative act or statute descended from Heaven as the basis for administering God's presence and blessings to His people in a given time. The Lord is basically saying to David that He is constantly having to move and develop from one system or set of protocols for manifesting himself (His presence-with-us) to another, in much the same way that the ordinance of the tabernacle of Moses was revised and updated in the tent of David, and again in Solomon's Temple.

The ordinance of Solomon's Temple was further revised during the period of Babylonian captivity when there was no visible temple as such; the Lord improvising nonetheless by that invisible temple of faith and grace through which the heavens were opened, worship was ensured, and salvation/instruction delivered to the children of God by men like Ezekiel and Daniel.

The ordinance of grace and worship was changed further, i.e., the Lord continues to move from tent to tent, and from one tabernacle to another, until eventually we come to the Son of man, the Temple that was destroyed and re-erected after three days. Of this temple we are told in John 1:14 that "the word was made flesh, and dwelt among us, (and we beheld his glory, the glory as of the only begotten of the Father) full of grace and truth." The word "dwelt" used in this verse describes the same situation as when used in the Old Testament injunction to Moses: "Let them build me a tabernacle that I may dwell among them."

This scenario of the development of the persistent purpose of God in Christ, i.e., the Way of Salvation, is brought out in these Seven Overcomeths, and each progressive *overcometh* typifies and signifies a dynamic updating of the ordinance of God's grace from the former state until the 'tabernacle' or *overcometh*/ordinance-of-grace that yields the fullness of Christ is reached or attained. In practical terms we will find, if we are moving on with the Lord, that from time to time there is a change of orientation and emphasis in His dealings with us that demands at each stage a corresponding development of faith, holiness, and power, as to our walk with Him and our service. This experience ties in with what is presented in the Seven Overcomeths which signify a practical expansion unto the spiritual majority of the fullness of Christ.

Before we actually begin to consider these *overcomeths*, let us examine aspects of the prefatory vision.

WHAT THOU SEEST WRITE IN A BOOK

"I John, who also am your brother, and companion in tribulation, and in the kingdom and patience of Jesus Christ, was in the isle that is called Patmos, for the word of God, and for the testimony of Jesus Christ. I was in the Spirit on the Lord's day, and heard behind me a great voice, as of a trumpet, saying, I am Alpha and Omega, the first and the last: and what thou seest, write in a book, and send it unto the seven churches which are in Asia, unto Ephesus, and unto Smyrna, and unto Pergamos, and unto Thyatira, and unto Sardis, and unto Philadelphia, and unto Laodicea. And I turned to see the voice that spake with me. And being turned, I saw seven golden candlesticks." (Revelation 1:9-12)

Let us first point out that John was a man bound up with the obligation to deliver and publish the Word of God, which is indeed the highest service. This obligation eventually meant that he would find himself estranged from his familiar environs, an exile in a solitary place, even as he himself has told us: "I John... was in the isle that is called Patmos, for the word of God, and for the testimony of Jesus Christ."

This obligation to establish the word of God for the children of God is brought out again by the injunction of the voice like a trumpet: "What thou seest, write in a book, and send it unto the seven churches." Or, in other words, "Write the vision, and make it plain upon tables, that he may run that readeth it."

The scenario presented here describes the highest service which is the ministry of the word of God. By this, I refer not to the preaching or teaching of the word, but to the primary function of seeing and hearing the 'vision' of knowledge and inscribing same in a 'book' that can be taken from place to place to form the basis of doctrine, study, preaching and general exhortation; setting down the nature and ordinance of the grace of God delivered, and the parameters and protocols by which this grace should become integrated and ingrained in the children of God who are the beneficiaries.

Furthermore, even as Moses, having ascended the mount to receive the word of God for Israel, descended to present that word enshrined in the structure, articles, and ordinance, of the physical tabernacle in the wilderness, so also John is given to describe the word of God for the saints through the symbolism of the Seven Churches (the tabernacle in the wilderness described through its structures, articles, and ordinance, the way of salvation unto the fullness of grace -- from the Gate of the Court through the Door of the Tent, and onto the Vail of the Holiest).

John tells us that as he turns to gaze upon the symbolic of the Word he comes face to face with the symbolic of the Seven Churches: "And I turned to see the voice that spake with me. And being turned, I saw seven golden candlesticks." (Revelation 1:12) As we consider this matter of the Seven Churches further, we shall discover that the symbolic is a representation of the Word of God delivered to the children of God, and the iterative *overcomeths* present to us the dynamic updating of the ordinance of His grace as He takes us from tent to tent, and from one tabernacle of His glorious presence to another.

Finally, as we conclude this preface to the Seven Churches (with Seven Overcomeths in tow) let us examine the latter part of the glorious vision of the exalted Christ as He appeared to John and commissioned him to set down the Word of Truth.

"Write the things which thou hast seen, and

the things which are, and the things which shall be hereafter; The mystery of the seven stars which thou sawest in my right hand, and the seven golden candlesticks. The seven stars are the angels of the seven churches: and the seven candlesticks which thou sawest are the seven churches." (Revelation 1:19-20)

Even as the shining cloud of the glory of God anointed and illuminated the erstwhile tabernacle of Moses and the Spirit of Truth must himself always set alight and illumine the letter of the word, so also the stars which are the angels of the churches bring the light and power that automate and activate the grace and truth as enshrined in the symbolic of the seven churches. We may now consider the seven churches -- the seven spiritual capacitors that yield the fullness of God's glories in Christ.

EPHESUS - SALVATION

(Revelation 2:1-7)

"Unto the angel of the church of Ephesus write; These things saith he that holdeth the seven stars in his right hand, who walketh in the midst of the seven golden candlesticks; I know thy works, and thy labor, and thy patience, and how thou canst not bear them which are evil: and thou hast tried them which say they are apostles and are not, and hast found them liars: And hast borne, and hast patience and for my name's sake hast labored, and hast not fainted.

Nevertheless, I have somewhat against thee because thou hast left thy first love. Remember therefore from whence thou art fallen, and repent, and do the first works; or else I will come unto thee quickly, and will remove thy candlestick out of his place, except thou repent. But this thou hast, that thou hatest the deeds of the Nicolaitanes, which I also hate. He that hath an ear, let him hear what the Spirit saith unto the churches; To him that overcometh will I give to eat of the tree of life, which is in the midst of the paradise of God."

In Ephesus we have all the elements from start to finish of the beginnings of a spiritual journey. In the salutation, we are instructed as from "he that holdeth the seven stars in his right hand," i.e., the light that has first shone through - the light of our salvation. After this, there is all the confusion of the mixed elements that started this journey along with us, i.e., the struggles between light and darkness -- "how thou canst not bear them which are evil: and thou hast tried them which say they are apostles, and are not, and hast found them liars."

This is reminiscent of all the initial struggle and unsettlement that arose in the camp of Israel immediately after their exodus from Egyptian bondage, i.e., their deliverance and salvation. We are told that a mixed multitude followed Moses out of Egypt, and the tussles for power and supremacy began at this point.

However, in Ephesus, because of the efforts to preserve the grace, the light that has come in, there is a quest to institutionalize this grace in order to save it from corruption, which quest ultimately leads to a situation of lethargy, formalism, and legalism, to the extent that the light is for the most part obscured. The warning then comes to recover the "first love" before the light is removed in totality.

Finally, there is the promise: "to him that overcometh"; he that is worthy to be accredited with the fruit of the tree of life, which is salvation. Hence, the church of Ephesus is that moral station of grace where the question of the resiliency of our salvation in Christ is answered one way or the other; how the light we first received is preserved through the doctrinal journeys, the theological controversies, the lethargic and formalistic trends, and last of all, through time, with its demands for patience and perseverance in waiting. Ephesus speaks of our salvation in Christ standing the test of time, and the peculiar accommodation accorded us by God's unique presence in our lives at this time.

SMYRNA - TEMPTATION
(Revelation 2:8-11)

"And unto the angel of the church in Smyrna write; These things saith the first and the last, which was dead, and is alive; I know thy works, and tribulation, and poverty, (but thou art rich) and I know the blasphemy of them which say they are Jews, and are not, but are the synagogue of Satan. Fear none of these things which thou shalt suffer: behold, the devil shall cast some of you into prison, that ye may be tried; and ye shall have tribulation ten days: be thou faithful unto death, and I will give thee a crown of life. He that hath an ear, let him hear what the Spirit saith unto the churches; he that overcometh shall not be hurt of the second death."

In Smyrna the word death occurs three times. The first is at the beginning in the salutation - "These things saith the first and the last, which was dead, and is alive." The second time is where the verse reads: "be thou faithful unto death, and I will give thee a crown of life." The third, and final, time is the promise to the overcomer which reads: "He that overcometh shall not be hurt of the second death."

Now, from start to finish, the character of this church is temptation. Our Lord provides indication of this when He speaks of himself as "he that was dead, and is alive." In other words, here, His accommodation and his grace to us will be in accordance with the dominant theme of this moral station which is temptation and suffering. It is almost as if the Lord has given us up to the devil's power and withdrawn himself. It's almost as if the Lord stands aloof, not really offering much help except to advise us to "fear none of those things which thou shalt suffer: behold, the devil shall cast some of you into prison, that ye may be tried; and ye shall have tribulation ten days."

It seems rather awkward when we put this passage against so much that is preached, taught, and believed, today in churches concerning how unusual it is for a Christian to suffer shameful and demeaning circumstances. We have heard the sayings oft repeated that this should not have happened to a Christian and that should not have happened to a Christian until we have become confused and bemused as we find ourselves overwhelmed and wrapped up in a cloud of oppression and crushing conditions. We are tempted to think (and people will help us along in this line of thought) that perhaps we have sinned against the Lord and this is why we are overwhelmed by such dark clouds of oppression.

Brethren, if you are moving on with God, after salvation the next step in your experience is temptation, and the Lord has ordained that a particular aspect of His grace and presence abide with you here. The Lord might seem to stand aloof, obscure, and detached, while all the encouragement you get is the constant impetus to not give up, to not be crushed and weighed down by the darkness around and the lack of understanding from those you expected to understand better. Peter elaborates on this in 1 Peter 4:12-19.

> "Beloved, think it not strange concerning the fiery trial which is to try you, as though some strange thing happened unto you... For the time is come that judgment must begin at the house of God: and if it first begin at us, what shall the end

be of them that obey not the gospel."

Smyrna, speaks of that sphere of His presence after salvation when He comes to us and leads us not only from Egypt, but into the wilderness to be tempted by the devil. Remember that our Lord Jesus came from the blessedness of Jordan's regenerating waters and a blissful experience of the Holy Ghost only to be driven into the wilderness to be tempted by Satan. He fasted forty days and forty nights until he finally became hungry. But in his hunger he found himself in the most unlikely place to find sustenance: the wilderness. Nor did he have an assistant, as did Moses, who could have helped him find relief. Without strength to help himself he could have died there out of weakness and starvation, and with a rebellious heart cursing God. It was at this point that Satan came and taunted him.

Satan teased and taunted him about his inability to help himself and how his God had led him into that situation, but Jesus drew his strength from the presence until finally, Satan departed, and the angels of God came and provided him with food almost when he should have succumbed to starvation.

Finally, we are told that "He that overcometh shall not be hurt of the second death." Those who shall avail themselves fully of the grace of this tabernacle, and so prevail against the tide of temptation and testing, shall be called the sons of God, and shall rule and reign with Christ escaping the final judgment which is the lake of fire.

PERGAMOS - BREAKING OF COVENANTS
(Revelation 2:12-17)

"And to the angel of the church in Pergamos write; These things saith he which hath the sharp sword with two edges; I know thy works, and where thou dwellest, even where Satan's seat is; and thou holdest fast my name, and hast not denied my faith, even in those days wherein Antipas was my faithful martyr, who was slain among you where Satan dwelleth. But I have a few things against thee, because thou hast there them that hold the doctrine of Balaam, who taught Balac to cast a stumblingblock before the children of Israel, to eat things sacrificed to idols, and to commit fornication. So hast thou also them that hold the doctrine of the Nicolaitanes, which thing I hate, Repent; or else I will come unto thee quickly, and will fight against them with the sword of my mouth. He that hath an ear, let him hear what the Spirit saith unto the churches; To him that overcometh will I give to eat of the hidden manna, and will give him a white stone, and in the stone a new name written, which no man knoweth saving he that receiveth it."

At this tabernacle or station of God's presence, we encounter the scourge of the Word of God - the sharp sword with two edges - to begin the work of purification and purging in us. Hebrews 4:12 tells us: "For the word of

God is quick, and powerful, and sharper than any two-edged sword, piercing even to the dividing asunder of soul and spirit, and of the joints and marrow, and is a discerner of the thoughts and intents of the heart."

This entrance of the Word of God in Pergamos is necessary because here the Lord begins in earnest His work of purging out all the dross from us, and preparing us for the glory that is to come.

We see that the covenant of peace and holiness the Lord established in us has been violated because of the doctrine of Balaam and his stumbling block. What is the stumbling block of Balaam? Of course, we have all read the story in the book of Numbers. But where does it find its application today? And how is this spiritual fornication accomplished, and the eating of things sacrificed unto idols?

Recently a relative, an elderly Efik lady, invited me to attend the ceremony of her conferment with the title of tribal chief in accordance with Efik tradition. This lady is also an elder in an evangelical church, and to all appearances is a decent, God-fearing, woman.

It was a lush ceremony which saw her enrobed in accessorized Efik attire and in full conformance with native custom, representative of the supplicative superstitions of Efik mystical tradition. Guests, many of whom were elders or officers of one church or another, joined themselves without reservation to every detail of the proceedings notwithstanding that some of the details were clearly averse to the Spirit and teaching of the Scriptures. This is an example of the doctrine of Balaam: the mingling together and confusing of social custom and tradition with Christian religious ceremony.

Other examples of the doctrine of Balaam are certain aspects of the traditional marriage ceremony observed and practiced in West Africa and the Nigerian southeast in particular. In many instances, symbols of the tribal gods are adorned by the bride especially, in the form of accessorized headdresses and other regalia -- thereby supplanting the holiness of God. Christians practice this ceremony and presume to give God the glory for the worship of their tribal gods.

In the Western world, we have a plethora of such practices and ceremonies widely observed and accepted by Christians and non-Christians alike, and presumed to be harmless lore and social custom, but many of which have their roots and antecedents in the occult, and rituals which date back to antiquity.

An example of one such Western practice is Halloween, a widely celebrated festival every 31st day of October in the United States. Originating in Europe from old Celt pagan traditions, Halloween or 'All Hallows eve' was to commemorate the New Year beginning November 1 in honor of the Lord of the Dead. October 31 was considered the one day when the veil separating the dead from the living was its thinnest thus enabling fraternity between the spirit world and the material world, hence the choice of that day. It was believed that at midnight this fraternity would peak, and so local Celts would dress up in ghoulish and ghostly costumes to facilitate fellowship with otherworldly spirits. Many modern-day witches in the West still hold October 31 as a day for the performance of important rituals.

In America there is a frenzied observance of the Halloween festival that is absolutely stunning to behold. Churches, both mainline denominational and newfangled evangelical, sponsor this festival with feverish gusto. Places of business are not exempted and compete in the glamour of their internal Halloween programs. I recall the first time I witnessed this festival. As I walked into my place of work in the Dallas Metroplex and strode down the aisle to my cubicle I observed with a chill in my spine how the entire office space was adorned with witchcraft paraphernalia: coffins, tombstones, webbing, effigies of witches, ghosts, skeletons, etc. People who profess Christ, attend and organize Bible studies, etc., and speak of waiting for the "Rapture" participate in these openly occult practices and frown at you for not joining them in their abomination. This is another prime example of the doctrine of Balaam and eating things sacrificed to idols that the Lord will have to separate us from before we can advance further down the path of salvation.

Throughout the history of the organized Church there has been a continuing enculturation of Christianity with pagan and worldly elements by un-Christ-like men who would adapt Christianity to make it more comfortable for them and their worldly peers. This is essentially the spiritual fornication and eating of things sacrificed to idols spoken of in Pergamos.

Another phenomenon that we would do well to take stock of at this juncture is the subtlety by which occult practice in general is making inroads into the social fabric of everyday life. This is as much a phenomenon affecting the more advanced West as it is in the less developed countries.

THE HARRY POTTER PHENOMENON

Sometime in 1990, a young British woman named J.K. Rowling found herself stuck on a train and decided to start writing. A decade later, her creation, Harry Potter, became arguably the UK's biggest cultural export ever. Harry Potter books have sold tens of millions of copies worldwide, and Harry himself, a boy magician schooled in the practice of witchcraft and sorcery has garnered somewhat of a cult following worldwide through his books and movies, avidly read and watched by children and adults alike.

By February 2002, Harry Potter books had generated such a surge of interest in sorcery and witchcraft that, amongst others, an Australian university was prompted to launch a special 12-week course open to the public upon which there came dozens of enquiries and enrollments.

Beyond education, Harry Potter's influence has also spread to healthcare delivery and into hospital wards. London's Great Ormond Street Hospital had by 2001 incorporated the use of this book in treating children with psychological difficulties and behavioral problems. The hospital used "Harry's magic" to devise a 'spell' to help children overcome their fear of needles. Clinical psychologists at Great Ormond Street, affirmed to BBC News that: "Harry Potter is useful in that children are aware of it. And where it has magic elements, it's very grounded in real things."

Presently, as this phenomenon consumes the minds of youth and adults worldwide through its books and movies, there is agitation amongst churches and social groups worldwide about the books' occult influence in captivating the minds of the youth and luring them towards the exploration and practice of witchcraft. Churches have burnt the books publicly and local communities have banned them from being sold in their bookstores. But these are very much in the minority, and taken to be knee-jerk reactions of superstitious people that do not appreciate art or good literature. However, this stands as another example of how the magnetism of social custom and trends entraps people into the doctrine of Balaam, to the extent that Satan is able to have a foothold on lives at a very early age requiring deliverance at later stages before such individuals can partake meaningfully of the grace of God in Christ Jesus.

In Nigeria, the surge in campus cult activity within the past three decades has signaled a dangerous revival of the occult and satanic ritual and practice among the youth which correlates to the global resurgence in occult activity, particularly among the youth.

The advent of civil rule in Nigeria in 1999 also acted as a catalyst to the resurgence of local occult ritual and practice as indigenous politics had more to do with the fervor of behind-the-scenes occult solicitations and their inherent Satanism than scientific politicking. As civil rule has progressed concurrently with extreme poverty and deprivation on the increase rather than on the decline, the desperation arising from failing state structures has led inevitably to even more fervent satanic and occult solicitation as a means for making inroads into the political sphere for sustenance as it were. Hence, the doctrine of Balaam has continued to make inroads into the fabric of social life making it even more necessary that we heed the voice of the Lord through His word for complete and total breaking of covenants and deliverance.

Another aspect worthy of consideration is the modernized version of the gospel that is retailed by mainline churches today. In particular the so-called prosperity and seed-faith messages, which are little more than crafty adaptations of Christian principles to suit the materialistic ideals of the high-brow and fast-lane mercantile world of today. This doctrine has invariably led to the perception amongst adherents that Church activity must needs revolve around and evince a show and ambience of wealth and affluence, to the extent that if a pastor is not affluent or wealthy he is in danger of losing credibility. As a result, cases are rampant of pastors engaging in criminal activities and scams to make money for "God's work" as it were and the adulation of the faithful. This is also the doctrine of Balaam.

Through all these unholy alliances and yokes the saints have compromised their heritage, and as such the glory of God cannot come close to them. Such covenants must be broken and a white stone with a new name given, signifying a new life; a spiritual renewal evincing a new covenant of surrender established between us and our Lord.

Several potentials of which we may be possessed have been by and large obscured and suppressed because of covenants we have knowingly or unknowingly entered into. At other times, we have entered these covenants due to certain acts performed on our behalf by our parents, aunts, uncles, etc. There are also covenants we enter into by virtue of marriage. These covenants militate against our progress, and are a stumbling block to our prayers and the manifestation of the grace of God in our lives. As such, they must be broken. This tabernacle of Pergamos is the beginning of our deliverance from the oppression of evil forces and their yokes which have nullified the grace of God in our lives.

Deliverance is a very important thing, and there is a

stage in our spiritual growth when, if we are obedient to the Lord, His dealings with us will center on this emphasis. He will begin at this point to root out and pull down, so that he can later build and plant. Deliverance is a very searching thing, and is no mean affair. Right at the very beginning of Pergamos we are confronted with the "sharp sword with two edges" which is a very searching thing. This sword will find us out as to our innermost constitution. Anything that is not planted by God in our lives must be rooted out, and this is always the nature of deliverance.

Deliverance can also be a humiliating experience as the Lord must take us down to the point where we are made to renounce and repudiate all evil and unholy associations, covenants, curses and what not. Some person or persons given to that ministry may be instrumental to this deliverance, or the Lord may employ extraordinary circumstances to achieve the desired result. But in any case, it must be done. The Lord's dealings with us in this tabernacle will center round deliverance and breaking of covenants.

In the rewards to the overcomer we see that he is given the hidden manna and a white stone with a new name. The white stone is a new testament or contract, and we remember that both the manna and the testimony were kept in the ark of the covenant of Moses, a symbol of the authority and the throne of God. So we see that after our deliverance we begin our equipment with real spiritual authority in heavenly places. Where in the past our prayers did not carry much weight, they are now very weighty because a measure of authority has been given. But this is just the beginning of our deliverance; there is another aspect that we must address as we progress from this tent of His presence to the next.

THYATIRA - INTERROGATION OF SPIRITS AND DELIVERANCE FROM WITCHCRAFT

(Revelation 2:18-29)

"And unto to the angel of the church in Thyatira write; These things saith the son of God, who hath his eyes like unto a flame of fire, and his feet are like fine brass; I know thy works, and charity, and service, and faith, and thy patience; and thy works; and the last to be more than the first. Notwithstanding I have a few things against thee, because thou sufferest that woman Jezebel, which calleth herself a prophetess, to teach and to seduce my servants to commit fornication, and to eat things sacrificed unto idols. And I gave her space to repent of her fornication; and she repented not. Behold, I will cast her into a bed and them that commit adultery with her into great tribulation, except they repent of their deeds. And I will kill her children with death; and all the churches shall know that I am he which searcheth the reins and hearts: and I will give unto everyone of you according to your works. But to you I say, and unto the rest in Thyatira, as many as have not this doctrine, and which have not known the depths of Satan, as they speak; I will put upon you none other burden. But that which ye have already hold fast till I come. And he that overcometh, and keepeth my works unto the end, to him will I give power over the nations: And he shall rule them with a rod of iron; as the vessels of a potter shall they be broken to shivers: even as I received of my father. And I will give him the morning star. He that hath an ear, let him hear what the spirit saith unto the churches."

At the tabernacle of Thyatira, the Lord's emphasis in His dealings with us again centers on deliverance. But in this case, our deliverance is not from the scourge of evil covenants, instead it is from the spirit of witchcraft.

I submit to you friends, that the most potent and powerful force designed by the enemy to hinder and frustrate the will and the grace of God in the lives of the saints is the spirit of witchcraft. In the above verses, reference is made to the woman Jezebel who calls herself a prophetess and causes the saints to stumble through spiritual fornication and eating of things sacrificed to idols. We have probably read the story of Jezebel in 1 Kings, and how she controlled all Israel with her witchcraft. But for the sovereign grace of God, she would have proved the utter undoing of that great prophet Elijah and all his work of reconciling the nation back to God.

We see the spirit of witchcraft again at work in Herodias, wife of Herod Antipas, and her diabolical designs on John the Baptist, symbol of the grace of God to Israel. She finally succeeds in manipulating the hand of the king to extinguish that bright and shining light, and John the Baptist suffers that terrible execution.

We see this power play again in the temple where these two opposing authorities -- the one of God and the other of the devil -- upon Jesus' triumphal entry into Jerusalem at the beginning of holy week, wrestle one against the other -- the power of God versus the diabolical machinations of the ruling Jewish council. And after Jesus drives out the money-changers and other miscreants, He is accosted by a delegation of the temple authorities with the question: "By whose authority doest thou these things?" In the exchange that follows, it is all a question of authority and what authority should predominate. A common feature of individuals that exercise this witchcraft influence in churches is their fetish of always having to be in total control of the church and of other people's lives. This is a manifestation of the spirit of witchcraft at work in the lives of Christians and churches.

It is a most sobering thing, and one that cannot be overstated, that the greatest hindrance the church, the body of Christ, will have in the performance of its ministry is this spirit of witchcraft that comes in various forms, and has suppressed and possessed men and women who pass so easily as bona fide believers, especially due to the widespread charismatic doctrines of affected spirituality, speaking in tongues, etc.

This matter must be searched out and scrutinized carefully, as to what spirits we bring with us into the Assembly of God, either as possessing them or being possessed of them, and the Lord's presence at this point of our development has employed the resources pertinent to this cause as He himself declares in the following verse:

"These things saith the son of God, who hath his eyes like unto a flame of fire, and his feet are like fine brass... and all the churches shall know that I am he which searcheth the reins and hearts..."

The Presence will employ these elements -- the eyes like a fiery flame and the feet like fine brass -- to scrutinize us and bring to light any spirit that is contrary to the Spirit of God, and to the Truth. Remember the significance of brass in the Old Testament? It was used in the furnishings of the tabernacle and the temple, and was associated with fire. It appears again in Ezekiel's vision of the temple in Ezekiel chapter 40 where he makes mention of the man of brass who stood at the entrance to the great vision. (Ezekiel 40:3) We see brass again in Revelation the first chapter when we rest our gaze on the portrait of the exalted Christ, and John tells us "And his feet like unto fine brass, as if they burned in a furnace." (Rev. 1:15)

Brass speaks of scrutiny and interrogation by the

holiness of God; that aspect of God's judgment that must take us apart and examine our every motive and very essence to verify complete obedience to His will. This is the work of deliverance that is effected in us at Thyatira.

Oppression by witchcraft also comes in here because all witchcraft influence in our lives must be subdued before we can optimally discharge our service, and perform our work of faith victoriously. This is why the reward to the overcomer here is power over the nations - power over "the rulers of the darkness of this world, spiritual wickedness (witchcraft) in high places." (Ephesians 6:12)

ANCESTRAL SPIRITS

One aspect of witchcraft oppression that we would do well to examine is the concept of ancestral spirits. This has become necessary because there is a whole slew of dreams and other spiritual experiences we have that are difficult to understand without delving into the realm from which these dreams and experiences take their shape and form, which is the traditional belief and practice, particularly in Africa, of the worship and veneration of ancestors and its effect and influence on younger generations including those who purport to embrace Christianity.

I knew of a young girl in southeast Nigeria who died of a sudden illness and as the hours passed, mourners came and went, and preparations were made for her embalming and burial, she miraculously revived and was taken up alive. She later recounted a story of how she was separated from her body in death and was transported to another country (as it seemed to her) where she was received by relatives whom she did not know and some whom she did. It was a fascinating place where people lived, worked, and carried on much as they did on the earth. Eventually, she was accosted by an elder of her family who asked her what she was doing there and what was the condition of her family on the earth. He appeared very agitated over the fact she ought not have been there at that time, and proceeded to drive her away with a stick. It was as she fled from him that she eventually awoke in her body and was taken up alive. When she described this person to her family, he was recognized to be one of the elders of the family who had passed away several years earlier.

On one of my trips to my own native village in Boki Local Government Area of Cross River State, I visited the home of one of my uncles as I strode through the village. As my uncle sat outside and cooked over his firewood hearth, he pointed behind me to his "father". I turned around but saw no-one. Puzzled, I asked, "Where is he?" He pointed again, and it was then I realized he was pointing to a tomb that was actually part of the pavement that stretched across the entrance to his house. As far as he was concerned, his father was still present but in a different form watching over him and his household. This is the way people are buried in mine and some other areas in Southeastern Nigeria. In some cases people are buried in

136

the floor of the house or bedroom. And the idea, again, is that these people are still living but on another plane. They have either become or are becoming ancestors and in any event are now part of the prevailing cosmogony enveloping the community and which inadvertently becomes a part of their dream world and related spiritual experiences.

In traditional religion, ancestors are the lubricant that ensures harmony in communal life. They appear in dreams and offer advice to herbalists and native healers in the use of herbs and other natural sciences that enable the community to survive. When clan members "go private", i.e. disregard their social responsibility by refusing to abide by the ritual and practice of the tribe, it is the ancestors that initiate retribution and punishments on them, and can also be invoked to visit punishment on erring clan members.

Upon the advent of Christian missions in Nigeria between the 18th and 19th centuries, there was not an immediate seismic shift in local religious thought and practice as foreign missions were not spiritually invasive but largely an extension of colonial machinations to facilitate enculturation of indigenous thought and practice with Western ideas and tastes to make it easier for the British Crown to exploit the resources of indigenous peoples and provide more effective administration of the Crown Colonies. But by the end of the 19th century when indigenous church formations and prayer groups began to break away, primarily from the Church Missionary Society, CMS, (the missionary arm of the Anglican Church) in Southwest Nigeria, and Pentecostal churches began to be formed things changed dramatically as a more dynamic and spiritually invasive type of faith was prosecuted. The first Indigenous churches were the Aladura, Christ Apostolic Church, Cherubim and Seraphim, and later the Celestial Church of Christ. Of these, the Christ Apostolic Church, was the more beholden to the study and practice of the scriptures, whilst the others were prone to syncretism to the extent that they did not have nor promoted a sound knowledge of the Bible.

At the time a prayer group, CAC in 1922 broke away from CMS (the Anglican Church's evangelical wing) joining first Faith Tabernacle, an American sect which practiced faith healing, then the British Apostolic Church, a Pentecostal church, finally becoming an independent church in 1941, taking the name Christ Apostolic Church. During this period, the British Apostolic Church sent missionaries, notable of which was the late S.G. Elton, to help consolidate the work of God. From the spiritual loins of S.G. Elton, fondly called Pa Elton, and the indigenous revivalists was spawned a confluence of Pentecostal streams that has since generated an expansion of Christianity in Nigeria and Africa almost unparalleled since the days of the first Apostles, to the extent that today historians are of the consensus that the center of gravity of Christianity has shifted from the West (i.e.

America and Europe, now regarded as the post-Christian West) to Africa, Latin America, and the Far Eastern countries.

What this has meant invariably for Christian practitioners in Africa primarily is that there has been a generational shift from the traditional African *outward* modes of worship as incompatible with Christian doctrine and practice -- whilst on the one hand, in many cases, there has not been as decisive a departure from *inward* modes of worship and experience as regards enchantment, witchcraft, and solicitation of (and oppression by) ancestral spirits. On the other hand, whilst there might have been somewhat of a spiritual separation from *inward* associations with tribal cults (by faith and affirmations), there are the almost unending tales of affliction by barrenness, broken homes, and general malaise in life and progress. These are the areas that the Lord is saying through Thyatira must be broken and a total separation made in order to give victory and the moral grace to advance further up the ladder to apprehend the full salvation in Christ.

Some persons, while living, have dreams of either themselves or others laboring as slaves in the factories or plantations of other unidentified -- or sometimes clearly discernible -- persons who may themselves be either dead or living. As a result, all their labor in the material world achieves for them no discernible benefit or meaningful progress. Others, having married against the wishes of the family or clan or otherwise failed to perform some required traditional ritual thereby offending the ancestors are the subject of concerted spiritual attacks in dreams by persons trying all ways to ambush and ultimately kill them. These are all manifestations of ancestral spirits wreaking havoc on those who purport to have faith in Christ.

Deliverance is an absolute necessity my brethren. Those who advocate simple indoctrination in the word of God as a remedy against these afflictions simply do not know what they are talking about.

Jesus performed deliverance on his disciples. He took them through mystical experiences that were designed to re-orientate, purge, and prepare them for the work he had called them to do and obtaining the full salvation. The transfiguration, the washing of the feet, the great intercessory prayer of John 17 in the garden of Gethsemane, and the 40 days' internship and empowerment between Jesus' resurrection and ascension were spiritual exercises designed to separate the disciples from any influences that may mitigate the resiliency of their faith and progress.

In our case prayer in the Spirit is the key, most effectively done by two, three, or more (i.e. where two or three are gathered together in my name…"). Sometimes deliverance may require that we visit our village or family home and perform prayers of recovery (of that which was lost). At other times, we may find that after spiritual prayer we visit those places in our dreams where, almost imperceptibly, the work of recovery is also done.

When we encounter spiritual wickedness and emerge triumphant we become more spiritual in nature and consistency, more sensitive and susceptible to spiritual things, and this is why we are given the morning star; we are given the ability to be truly spiritual beings that war and have their discourse in the spiritual realm.

SARDIS – SANCTIFICATION AND COMMENDATION TO GOD'S GRACE AND THE ELECT ANGELS

(Revelation 3:1-6)

"And unto the angel of the church in Sardis write; These things saith he that hath the seven spirits of God, and the seven stars; I know thy works, that thou hast a name that thou livest, and art dead. Be watchful, and strengthen the things which remain, that are ready to die: for I have not found thy works perfect before God. Remember therefore how thou hast received and heard, and hold fast, and repent. If therefore thou shalt not watch, I will come on thee as a thief, and thou shalt not know what hour I will come upon thee. Thou hast a few names even in Sardis which have not defiled their garments; and they shall walk with me in white: for they are worthy. He that overcometh, the same shall be clothed in white raiment; and I will not blot out his name out of the book of life, but I will confess his name before my Father, and before his angels. He that hath an ear, let him hear what the spirit saith unto the churches."

The tabernacle or spiritual station of Sardis is for the preparation and adornment of the panoply of spiritual power for active service. All the stages through which we have passed with regard to our deliverance and purging through Pergamos and Thyatira were to prepare and make us ready for Sardis, where we receive the ordination for service by a ceremonial array of the panoply or mantle of power.

Let us examine some of the key words in this passage.

"These things saith he that hath the seven spirits of God, and the seven stars." This phrase refers to the array of elect angels that are to be commissioned to stand at the behest of the sanctified children of God. The seven spirits of God and the seven stars here signify the angelic host given to confirm and establish a specific campaign or ministry of the kingdom of God.

"Thou hast a few names in Sardis that have not defiled their garments; and they shall walk with me in white: for they are worthy."

Here again, we see the result of our deliverance yielding a readiness for service - "They have not defiled their garments and are now worthy to walk with me in white." At this point we are now ready for our spiritual service or ministry; we have been sanctified by the work of deliverance in us and we are ready to perform our service optimally. The wearing of white always speaks of the resultant work of our personal sanctification which makes us ready to undertake a serious spiritual campaign.

"He that overcometh, the same shall be clothed in white raiment; and I will not blot out his name out of the book of life, but I will confess his name before my Father, and before his angels."

In answer to this verse, let us turn to a situation in the closing hours of Jesus' life on earth which accurately parallels what we have here. At this time of Jesus' ministry with the disciples, the $3^{1/2}$-year period of their internship and probation is nearing its end. During this period, Jesus has taken them from one sanctifying/cleansing work of deliverance to another, eventually culminating in the sacrament of the washing of feet after the last supper. (John 13:11) In fact, at this very point Peter attempts to avoid this matter by stating, rather piously, that the Lord should never wash his feet. To which Jesus replies, "If I wash thee not, thou hast no part with me." Peter would have no part in the grace that was to be given them for service unless he partook of this last sacrament of deliverance.

Subsequently, as they strolled together in the garden,

having done all to prepare and make ready the little flock the Father had given him, Jesus prayed that great intercessory prayer in John chapter 17 where he commends His disciples to God's grace and removes the panoply of power from himself as it were, and places it on His disciples. "And the glory which thou gavest me I have given to them; that they may be one, even as we are one." It is a beautiful passage if you read the entire chapter from start to finish, and it illustrates clearly and vividly what we have here in Sardis where it is said: "I will confess his name before my Father, and before his angels." This is the place in our spiritual development where we are introduced to the host of elect angels and to the panoply of power for authority in service, so that these elements of God's kingdom will reinforce our ministry, establishing our word and our actions.

In Sardis there is a culmination of the training and discipline though which we must pass as children of God in order to become fully endowed with our spiritual fullness for service. Having passed through all the stages of sanctification and purification, the glory of God can now come close to us and we are fully equipped with heavenly authority for service.

The two remaining tabernacles, Philadelphia and Laodicea, describe specific issues of grace and power to be given to an elect group of victorious and holy believers in the closing stages of this age, when the challenges of the antichrist's war with the saints will have reached a climax. This time is generally described as the Great Tribulation, and these are specific issues of grace and power to be released to the holy ones to carry them over and through this tide of trouble. These two remaining tabernacles are for that "glorious church without spot or wrinkle, or any such thing; but holy and without blemish."

(Ephesians 5:27)

Let us now consider Philadelphia.

PHILADELPHIA - THE OPEN HEAVEN OF POWER AND DESCENDING OF THE CHAPEL OF GRACE
(Revelation 3:7-12)

"And unto the angel of the church in Philadelphia write; These things saith he that is holy, he that is true, he that hath the key of David, he that openeth, and no man shutteth: and shutteth, and no man openeth; I know thy works: behold I have set before thee an open door, and no man can shut it: for thou hast a little strength, and hast kept my word, and hast not denied my name. Behold, I will make them of the synagogue of Satan, which say they are Jews, and are not, but do lie; behold, I will make them to come and worship before thy feet, and to know that I have loved thee. Because thou hast kept the word of my patience, I also will keep thee from the hour of temptation, which shall come upon all the world, to try them that dwell upon the earth.

Behold, I come quickly: hold that fast which thou hast, that no man take thy crown. Him that overcometh will I make a pillar in the temple of my God, and he shall go no more out: and I will write upon him the name of my God, and the name of the city of my God, which is new Jerusalem, which cometh down out of heaven from my God: and I will write upon him my new name. He that hath an ear, let him hear what the spirit saith unto churches."

Here in Philadelphia, as we said before, we have the issue of special grace and power by "he that is holy, he that is true" in the churches. "He that hath the key of David, he that openeth, and no man shutteth: and shutteth, and no man openeth." This grace is especially for those who have kept the word of His patience for safety and security from the ravages of the Great Tribulation. This grace is an open heaven of power into which the saints will be graduated; a chapel of grace embodying the functionality of that glorious church without spot or wrinkle, designed to make them victorious over every challenge, and eventually as we shall see when we consider Laodicea, over the last enemy which is death.

The open door spoken of in Philadelphia answers to the open heaven I have just described whose functionality is indicated in Revelation 4:1-2 where it says: "After this I looked, and behold, a door was opened in heaven: and the first voice which I heard was as it were of a trumpet talking with me; which said, come up hither, and I will shew thee things which must be hereafter. And immediately I was in the Spirit: and behold, a Throne was set in heaven, and one sat on the Throne." Hence this open door is an open heaven of power that puts us in direct relation to the Throne, and He who sits on the Throne.

Again, this functionality is described in Revelation 12:1-5 by the scenario of the woman with child travailing in birth, and the great red dragon crouched between her legs to devour her child as soon as it was born. All of a sudden, it says: "And she brought forth a man-child, who was to rule all nations with a rod of iron: and her child was caught up unto God, and to his throne."

The functionality of that open door is further described by the war in heaven between Michael and his angels, and the dragon and his angels, until eventually the dragon -- that old devil -- the accuser and tormentor of the saints is cast down from the heavenly realms. This pertains principally to the great persecution of the saints by the antichrist and the constant keeping in abeyance of the forces of evil on behalf of the little flock the saints will have the oversight of.

The temple of God, also called "the city of God, which is new Jerusalem, which cometh down out of heaven from my God" in Philadelphia is the chapel of grace, a lofty spiritual condition whose functionality is indicated in Revelation 21:2-4 where we are shown a preview of this chapel descending from heaven with a voice describing its functionality:

"Behold, the tabernacle of God is with men, and he will dwell with them, and they shall be his people, and God himself shall be with them, and be their God. And God shall wipe away all tears from their eyes; and there shall be no more death, neither sorrow, nor crying, neither shall there be any more pain."

There lies the functionality of the chapel of grace that descends upon the holy ones in Philadelphia; it is to equip them with power to wipe away the tears of their brethren, to frustrate death, and wipe away the sorrows of pain - all those things brought upon people as a result of the Great Tribulation. The elect few who will enter the tent of Philadelphia will save their brethren, a little flock that the Lord will give them, from the ravages of the Great Tribulation. This is the meaning of Philadelphia - it is prophetic.

LAODICEA - THE SECRET OF RESURRECTION POWER

(Revelation 3:14-21)

"And unto the angel of the church of the Laodiceans write; These things saith the Amen, the faithful and true witness, the beginning of the creation of God; I know thy works, that thou art neither cold nor hot: I would thou wert cold or hot. So then because thou art lukewarm, and neither cold nor hot, I will spue thee out of my mouth. Because thou sayest, I am rich, and increased with goods, and have need of nothing; and knowest not that thou art wretched, and miserable, and poor, and blind, and naked: I counsel thee to buy of me gold tried in the fire, that thou mayest be rich; and white raiment, that thou mayest be clothed, and that the shame of thy nakedness do not appear; and anoint thine eyes with eyesalve, that thou mayest see. As many as I love, I rebuke and chasten: be zealous therefore, and repent. Behold, I stand at the door, and knock, if any man hear my voice, and open the door, I will come in to him, and will sup with him, and he with me. To him that overcometh will I grant to sit with me in my throne, even as I also overcame, and am set down with my father in his throne. He that hath an ear, let him hear what the spirit saith unto the churches."

Laodicea offers to us the secret of resurrection power as possessed by our Lord and attainable by those chosen saints who graduate through the open door of Philadelphia. The background to this vision is found in the 42-month war the antichrist wages against the saints, and which spreads across the length and breadth of the globe. The Lord will give protection to the believers through the handful of holy ones that will have the open heaven to protect and shepherd those that will shelter under their wings. The faithful will keep the antichrist in abeyance until the time of temptation when they are provoked to apprehend the secret of resurrection power, and they destroy the last enemy which is death.

The salutation to Laodicea speaks of an irrefutable surety from the "Amen, the faithful and true witness, the beginning of the creation of God." Jesus is the beginning of the creation of God because he is the firstborn from the dead; He is the firstborn of a new creation of sons of God on the basis of their conquest of death and attainment of resurrection life and power. This resurrection power will be apprehended, or won, on the basis of those who shall be faithful and true witnesses. A faithful and true witness is a martyr, one who like Christ stands by his testimony even unto death. The wisdom that is here tells us that the secret of resurrection power lies somewhere in the manner by which one confirms his testimony for God; the manner and extent to which his will to serve God, his testimony of the word of God, and his willingness to be martyred, if necessary, for the sake of the word coincide and resemble Christ's in every aspect.

The apostle Paul realized this, and gave us that thought-provoking passage in Philippians 3:10-11.

> "That I may know him, and the power of his resurrection, and the fellowship of his sufferings, being made conformable unto his death; if by any means I might attain unto the resurrection of the dead."

This is what is presented to us here at Laodicea; the

conquest of the last enemy - death – by resurrection. The natural result of our Lord's resurrection was exaltation to the Throne of God, and the natural result of the attainment of resurrection power by the elect will be exaltation and seating in the throne of Christ, and this is brought out in the reward to the overcomer.

> "To him that overcometh will I grant to sit with me in my throne, even as I also overcame, and am set down with my Father in his throne."

Similarly, we find that the riches of gold tried in the fire, the white raiment for clothing, and the eye- ointment for sight, are all symbols of a resurrected body, a resurrected life, and we are enjoined to trade in our despicable and carnal life for these riches: "I counsel thee to buy of me..." But all this is in pains of death, and our Lord said as much when he admonished: "He that loveth his life shall lose it; and he that hateth his life in this world shall keep it unto life eternal." (John 12:25) Interestingly, He spoke these words whilst at the same time speaking of his impending death and resurrection from the dead. (John 12:20-28)

Made in the USA
Middletown, DE
24 April 2022

64701883R00086